IMAGES
of America

SAN RAMON
VALLEY

ALAMO, DANVILLE, AND SAN RAMON

Twenty years after statehood, the rural San Ramon Valley is depicted in this 1871 county map. The villages of Alamo and Danville have clusters of buildings and a square at the bottom shows the 4,500 acres of San Ramon land, which pioneer Leo Norris bought from Jose Maria Amador in 1850.

IMAGES
of America

SAN RAMON VALLEY

ALAMO, DANVILLE, AND SAN RAMON

Beverly Lane and Ralph Cozine for
the Museum of the San Ramon Valley

ARCADIA
PUBLISHING

Published by Arcadia Publishing
Charleston, South Carolina

Library of Congress Catalog Card Number: 2005932473

For all general information contact Arcadia Publishing at:
Telephone 843-853-2070
Fax 843-853-0044
E-mail sales@arcadiapublishing.com
For customer service and orders:
Toll-Free 1-888-313-2665

Visit us on the Internet at www.arcadiapublishing.com

Agriculture played an important role in San Ramon Valley history after the gold rush. Farms, ranches, and orchards dominated the landscape. This combine harvests grain on the hillside.

CONTENTS

ACKNOWLEDGMENTS

Although we did the research, writing, and collecting of photographs, many others helped us create this book. Our thanks to all.

Most of the images came from the archives of the Museum of the San Ramon Valley and the Contra Costa County Historical Society. Others were provided by Doug Aitken, the Bancroft Library, *Bay Nature* magazine, Bishop Ranch Business Park, the Bettencourt family, Betty and Paul Dunlap, Betty Casey, Al Davies, Forest Home Farms, Bill Hockins, Irma and Jim Dotson, Craig Lyon, Marilyn Lynch Morrison, Claudia Nemir, Peter Oswald, Egon Pedersen, Edna Lynch Scott, John Silveira, Lee Taylor, Roi Peers, SRV Fire Protection District, the Wiedemann family, and the Wood family.

In addition to these archives and individual donors, major sources of information for our captions include scrapbooks created by Roy Bloss, Irene M. Cordes, and Vivian Coats Edmonston. We used books and articles by Seth Adams, Inez Butz, Wilson Close, Irma M. Dotson, Rose Peters Emery, Virgie V. Jones, Barbara Hall Langlois, Robert Tatam, Charlotte Wood, and Don Wood. Other excellent help came from Bill Fereira, Kathy Fitzpatrick, Millie Freitas, Bill Hockins, Ann Kaplan, Roxanne Lindsay, Mount Diablo Interpretive Association, Mount Diablo State Park, George Stegemann, Studio Blue Digital Print and Copy, Jeff Wiedemann, county newspapers, the *Valley Pioneer,* and several Contra Costa County histories (1879, 1882, 1917, and 1940). For a list of other books about San Ramon Valley, please see page 128.

Special thanks to Irma M. Dotson for collecting historical photographs for over 25 years with help from the San Ramon Valley Historical Society. Thank you also to Marillyn Cozine, Jim Lane, and Betty Dunlap, who provided invaluable support for this book.

—Beverly Lane and Ralph Cozine
for the Museum of the San Ramon Valley

INTRODUCTION

These images tell the story of the beautiful San Ramon Valley. Located not far from San Francisco Bay at the base of Mount Diablo, the 20-mile valley includes commercial and civic centers, suburban homes, open spaces, and a major business park. Interstate 680 and the Iron Horse Regional Trail link the valley's original communities of Alamo, Danville, and San Ramon.

Much of valley history may be viewed as a microcosm of California. The area has an interesting geology and unusual prehistoric animals. The first residents, American Indians, lived in the valley for thousands of years. In 1772, the first Spaniards arrived, and, in the 1830s, two Mexican ranchos were established. California's mythic 1848 gold rush drew energetic pioneers from the eastern United States and countries throughout the world. Later Portuguese, Danish, Italian, Irish, and Japanese settlers came to the valley. After statehood was established in 1850, Mount Diablo became the initial point for public land surveys in most of California and all of Nevada (1851). Ranches and farms were set up around village centers and, until the 1960s, agriculture was the business of the valley.

This picture sampler focuses on the San Ramon Valley, an area with moderate weather, many parks, excellent schools, jobs, and proximity to all Northern California has to offer. As one booster newspaper wrote, "the land here will grow anything planted, and the climate makes one want to linger here forever." Once part of the distant rural edge of the Bay Area, today San Ramon, Dougherty Valley, Diablo, Danville, Blackhawk, and Alamo are integral parts of East Bay urban life.

SIGNIFICANT DATES IN VALLEY HISTORY

5,000 years ago	People lived in the San Ramon Valley.
1772	The first Spaniards explored the valley.
1797	Mission San Jose is founded, and mission livestock are grazed in the valley.
1833–1834	Two Mexican ranchos are granted in the valley.
1848	Gold is discovered in the Sierras.
1850	California becomes a state.
1850	Leo and Jane Norris and family and William Lynch move into San Ramon.
1851	Leander Ransom sets the initial point on Mount Diablo.
1852	The first post office is established in Alamo, with John M. Jones as postmaster.
1873	Danville Grange No. 85 is founded, led by worthy master Charles Wood.
1891	The San Ramon branch of the Southern Pacific opens.
1910	The first public high school is established.
1912	R. N. Burgess opens the Mount Diablo Park Club.
1914–1924	Electric railway serves Alamo, Danville and Mount Diablo Park Club.
1921	Mount Diablo State Park opens as a small game refuge.
1921	San Ramon Valley Fire Protection District is started.
1964	The I-680 freeway reaches Sycamore Valley Road in Danville.
1965	San Ramon Valley Unified School District is approved by voters.
1966	The freeway continues from Sycamore Valley Road to Dublin.
1966	Las Trampas Regional Wilderness first land purchase is made.
1978	Bishop Ranch Business Park is established.
1982–1983	Danville and San Ramon incorporate.
1997	San Ramon Valley Fire Protection District merges all valley fire districts.

Alhambra
Valley

Pacheco

Concord
(Todos Santos)

Pleasant
Hill

Reliez Valley

Ygnacio Valley

Cowell

Clayton

Norton-
ville

Somers-
ville

Empire
Mine

Stewarts-
ville

Judsonville

West Hartl

Briones
Reservoir

Lafayette

Walnut Creek

Orinda

Lafayette
Reservoir

Saranap

MT. DIABLO MERIDIAN

Mount
Diablo

MT. DIABLO BASE LINE

Tunnel

Canyon

Moraga

St. Mary's

Alamo

San Ramon Valley

Diablo

Morga
Territory

Danville

Tassajara

San Ramon

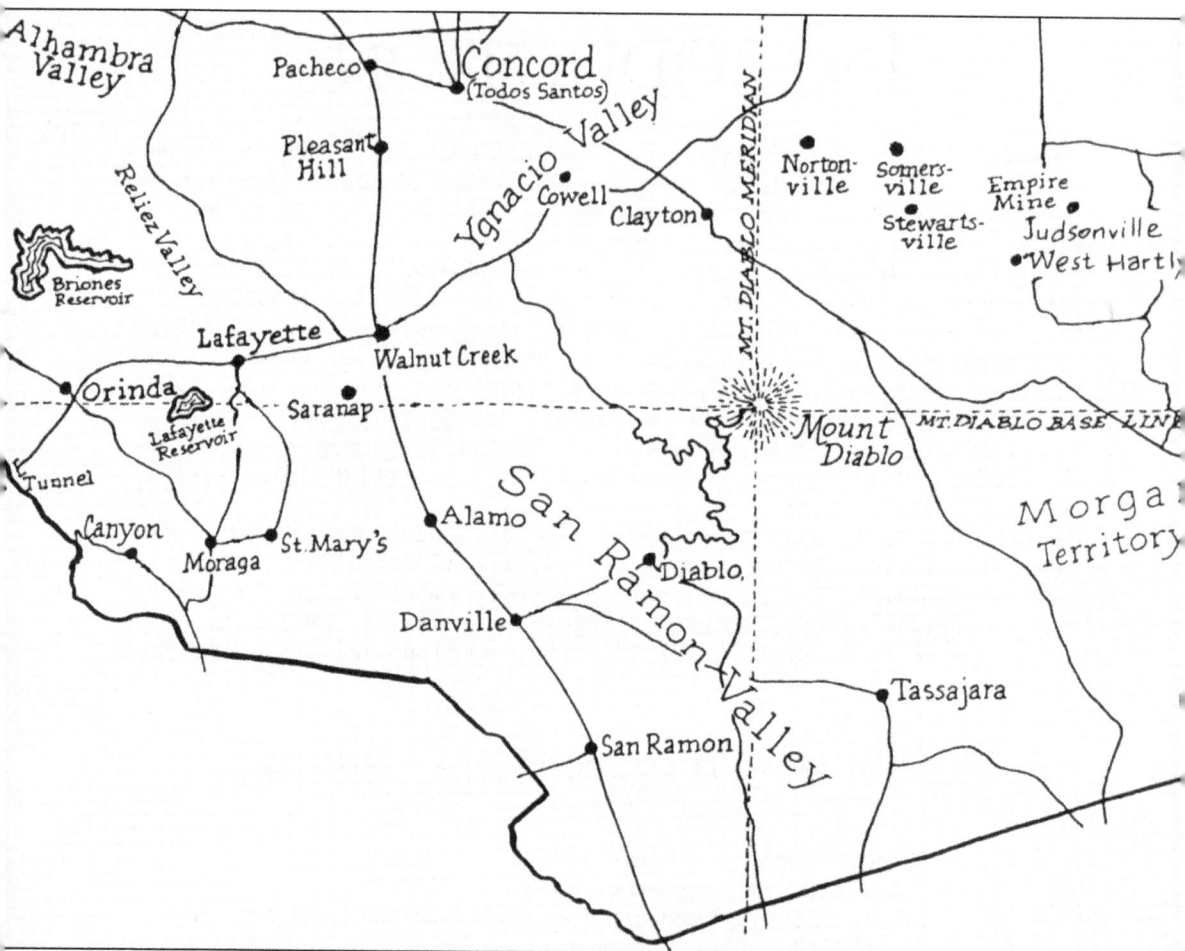

This map, modeled on one from Robert Tatam, locates the San Ramon Valley next to Mount
Diablo in California's southern Contra Costa County.

8

One

THE LANDMARK MOUNTAIN

Almost every Californian has seen Monte Diablo. It is the great central landmark of the state. Whether we are walking in the streets of San Francisco, or sailing on any of our bays and navigable rivers, or riding on any of the roads in the Sacramento and San Joaquin Valleys, or standing on the elevated ridges of the mining districts before us—in lonely boldness, and at almost every turn, we see Monte del Diablo.

—J. M. Hutchings, *Scenes of Wonder and Curiosity in California*, 1860

Mount Diablo rises 3,849 feet over the San Ramon Valley and other surrounding valleys. The mountain began to emerge as a topographic feature 2 million years ago and is still changing, as earthquakes along the Calaveras and Greenville faults attest. The view from the summit is extraordinary; on a clear day, the peaks of the Sierra and Yosemite's Half Dome can be seen to the east. A favorite destination for tourists and campers since statehood, visitors relish hiking, biking, and driving to the top.

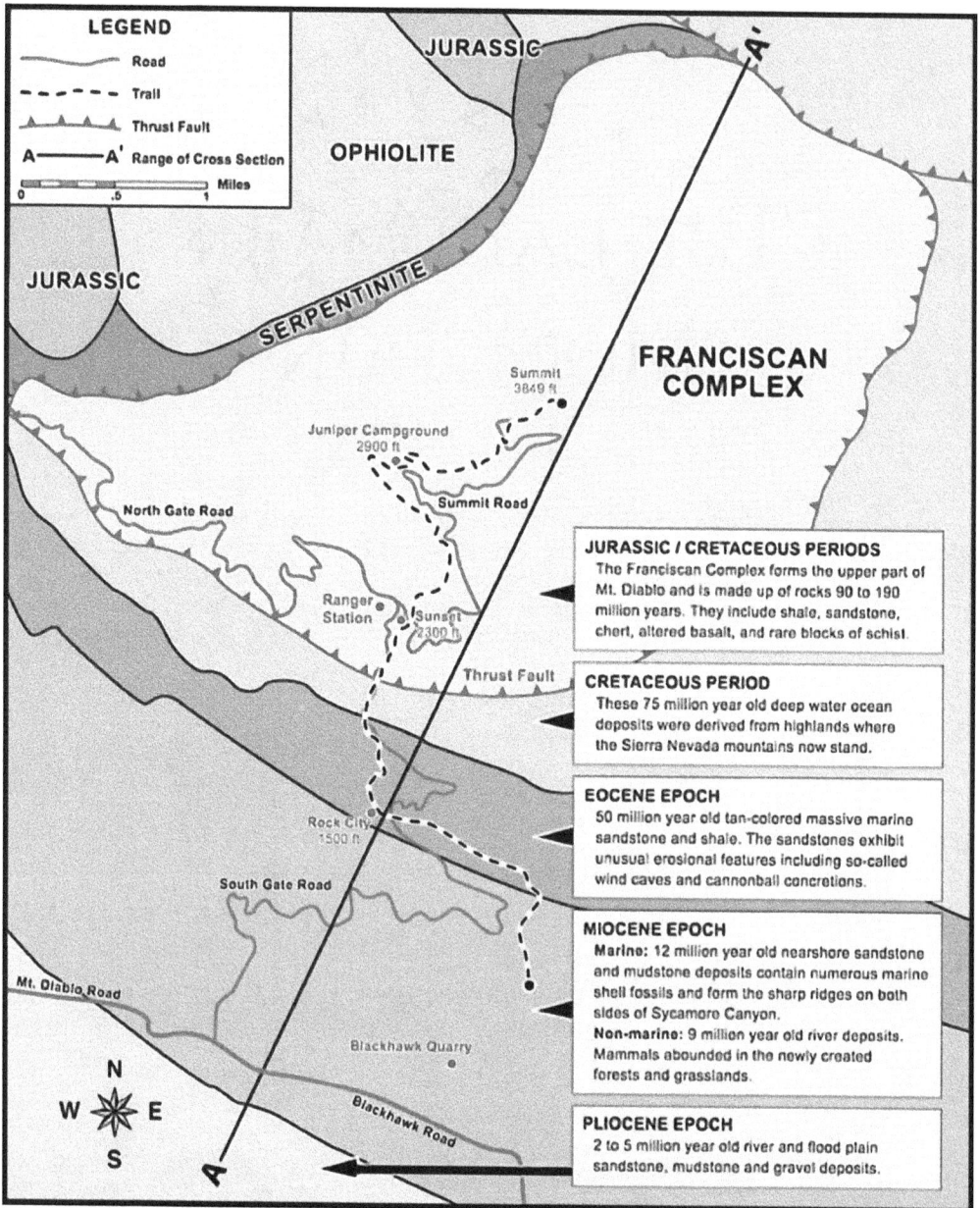

LEGEND

〰〰〰 Road

- - - - Trail

⩕⩕⩕⩕⩕ Thrust Fault

A———A' Range of Cross Section

0 .5 1 Miles

JURASSIC

OPHIOLITE

JURASSIC

SERPENTINITE

A'

FRANCISCAN COMPLEX

Summit
3849 ft

Juniper Campground
2900 ft

North Gate Road

Summit Road

Ranger
Station

Sunset
2300 ft

Thrust Fault

Rock City
1500 ft

South Gate Road

Mt. Diablo Road

Blackhawk Quarry

Blackhawk Road

N
W E
S

A

JURASSIC / CRETACEOUS PERIODS
The Franciscan Complex forms the upper part of Mt. Diablo and is made up of rocks 90 to 190 million years. They include shale, sandstone, chert, altered basalt, and rare blocks of schist.

CRETACEOUS PERIOD
These 75 million year old deep water ocean deposits were derived from highlands where the Sierra Nevada mountains now stand.

EOCENE EPOCH
50 million year old tan-colored massive marine sandstone and shale. The sandstones exhibit unusual erosional features including so-called wind caves and cannonball concretions.

MIOCENE EPOCH
Marine: 12 million year old nearshore sandstone and mudstone deposits contain numerous marine shell fossils and form the sharp ridges on both sides of Sycamore Canyon.
Non-marine: 9 million year old river deposits. Mammals abounded in the newly created forests and grasslands.

PLIOCENE EPOCH
2 to 5 million year old river and flood plain sandstone, mudstone and gravel deposits.

Mount Diablo has a complex geology composed of ancient rocks. The Farallon and North American Plates pushed together for millions of years, in an ongoing process called plate tectonics, and created the mountain. This drawing shows one of Mount Diablo State Park's interpretive panels, which traces the intriguing Trail Through Time.

In 1861 and 1862, the California State Geological Survey (known as the Whitney Survey) studied Mount Diablo. The 1864 field party, from left to right, was James T. Gardiner, Richard D. Cotter, William H. Brewer, and Clarence King. They examined the mountain's height, geology, and fossils and discovered 25 unknown plants. Brewer was in charge of botany and led the survey's fieldwork throughout California. His notebooks, botanical collections, drawings, and photographs are at the Jepson Herbarium, University of California, Berkeley.

At the Blackhawk Ranch fossil quarry, first discovered by Nestor John Sandor in 1937, fossils have been found from an unusual mastodon, the *Gomphotherium*. Other fossilized animals unearthed include saber-toothed cats (*Smilodon*), massive dogs (*Epicyon diabloensis*), three-toed horses (*Hipparion forcei*), camels (*Procamelus*), and large llamas (*Megatylopus*). In complexity and number of artifacts, the quarry is second in California only to Los Angeles's La Brea Tar Pits. Carl Buell painted this picture.

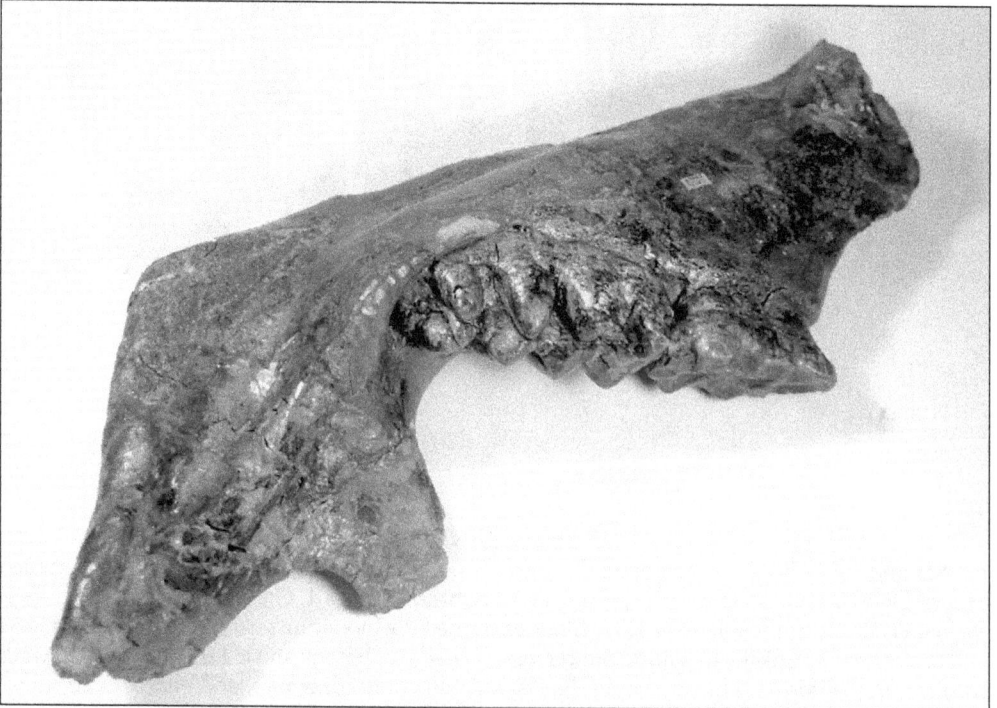

This fossilized mastodon jaw may be seen at the Museum of the San Ramon Valley, on loan from the University of California's Museum of Paleontology. A double-tusked vegetarian, the *Gomphotherium* mastodon appeared in northern California about 10 million years ago and disappeared about 10,000 years ago.

12

In 1851, Col. Leander Ransom, a U.S. deputy surveyor general, established the principal reference point for land surveys on Mount Diablo's peak. From this initial point, land in most of California and all of Nevada is surveyed. The state park built this platform for visitors to enjoy the summit's panoramic views.

This platform was a tourist destination for decades. In addition to Ransom's initial point, the U.S. Coast and Geodetic Survey used the Mount Diablo peak as a base point for its national triangulation survey in 1852.

After 1874, tourists were able to take Seeley Bennett's stage line from Martinez to Diablo's peak. The Mountain House Hotel servants' building is also shown. Stagecoaches provided some exciting trips up and down the mountain. One local stage line was Brown and Company, which traveled in 1864 between Walnut Creek and San Ramon, connected with the Oakland line, and stayed in the valleys.

On a visit to the mountain in 1920, this huge eagle was killed. Mount Diablo is home to the peregrine falcon and North America's largest spider, the tarantula. The mountain represents the northern limit of some plant species (e.g. Coulter pine) and the southern limit of others (e.g. Hooker's onion). Several plants found only on the mountain include the Mount Diablo globe tulip, manzanita, sunflower, and buckwheat. The man second from the left is Leo Norris of San Ramon.

14

Trips up the mountain to caves and glades were very popular. In front of this cave are the Woods of Sycamore Valley, from left to right, Charlotte, Howard, Waldo, unidentified, and Libbie.

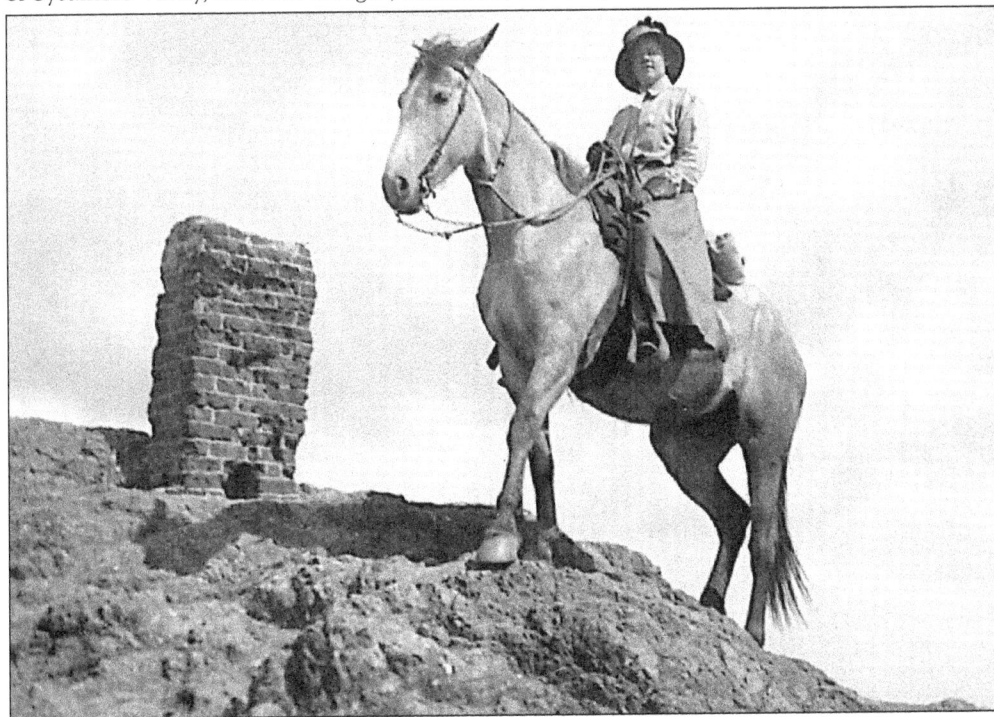

Mattie Wiedemann of San Ramon rides her horse to visit the brick column at the summit, early in the 20th century.

On June 19, 1921, a celebration marked the new park on Diablo's summit, presided over by Lt. Gov. C. C. Young. Mount Diablo State Park began as a 630-acre state park and game refuge without any public access. It was created by legislation sponsored by local state senator Will R. Sharkey. The park was one of seven state parks created before the California state park system was founded in 1927.

From 1912 to 1915, new auto toll roads to the Mount Diablo summit were constructed by R. N. Burgess, who produced nationwide publicity touting the mountain's views. The toll for an automobile with passengers was $1, for a six-horse vehicle the charge was $2.50, and for hikers 25¢. Bay Area visitors could take the new electric railway to the Mount Diablo Park Club and take a motor stage up the mountain.

16

Diablo Camp 1817
Photo by Davies Alamo, Cal.

In the 1930s, the Civilian Conservation Corps (CCC) constructed Camp Diablo on the San Ramon Valley side of the mountain and built new facilities throughout the park, including roads, trails, residences, picnic areas, campgrounds, and the visitor center. The corps helped improve the new state park when it was enlarged to 2,000 acres. In 1931, the park opened to the public.

Another CCC camp was built south of the park at the northeast corner of today's Camino Tasssajara and Old Blackhawk Road. Residents called this intersection Four Corners. During World War II, it became Camp San Ramon and provided mobilization training for special military training units. Later Italian internees were housed in the buildings.

In 1928, Standard Oil of California constructed a 75-foot tower with an aviation beacon to act as a guide for commercial aviation. Charles Lindberg first turned it on (from a remote location). The Standard Diablo beacon was later transferred to the visitor center. After December 7, 1941, the beacon was turned off; today it is illuminated annually on December 7 to commemorate Pearl Harbor.

In 1931, the state park was enlarged, and opened to the public. The Civilian Conservation Corps built the visitor center from 1939 to 1942 using rock quarried from the park's Fossil Ridge. This building is an excellent example of rustic park architecture. The summit museum features the park's ecosystems, geology, human history, and the original initial survey point. During winter, the mountaintop is often dusted with snow.

Two

EARLY TIMES

In 1770 the political landscape of the San Francisco Bay region was a mosaic of tiny tribal territories, each some eight to twelve miles in diameter . . . The Tatcans held the San Ramon Creek just west of Mount Diablo . . . The first large group went to Mission San Francisco in the first months of 1804. The Seunen and Souyen (south of Mount Diablo) went to Mission San Jose after 1797.

—Randall Milliken, A Time of Little Choice, 1995

These dancers, probably from the Tri-Valley area, were drawn by a Rezanov expedition artist, who visited Mission San Jose in 1806. When these Indians came to the mission, they brought dance regalia and traditional dances. People had lived in San Ramon Valley villages for at least 5,000 years. The Spanish invaded the valley in 1772, established Mission San Jose in 1797, and put cattle and sheep tended by Indian vaqueros on the land. Two Mexican ranchos were granted to former soldiers in the valley.

19

There were probably several villages in the San Ramon Valley, each with 50 to 150 people. The rhythm of the Indians' lives followed the seasons as they gathered seeds, acorns and soap root, burned grasses, hunted, and fished. They hosted autumn gatherings on the mountain and may have danced to keep the world in balance. Their houses and other structures, made from willow frames, were covered with grasses or tule, as illustrated by Al Greger.

Acorns were a rich source of food for the first people. Gathered by the entire village in the fall, acorn processing took time. Acorns were dried, cleaned, shelled, pounded, rinsed, and cooked in watertight baskets using hot stones. (Drawing by Bunner McFarland.)

Louis Choris sketched these American Indians in 1816 when he came to the San Francisco Bay. The figures on the right are two views of a Saclan woman who, like the Tatcan of northern San Ramon Valley, spoke a Bay Miwok language. Seunen and Souyen Indians, who spoke an Ohlone/Costanoan language, lived in today's San Ramon and Dublin areas in a watershed that led to huge marshes.

Baskets were called utensils in this 1816 drawing by Louis Choris since they served many purposes. They were used to gather and store food, carry wood, trap animals, and hold babies. Intricate designs and fine workmanship were characteristic of California Indian basketry.

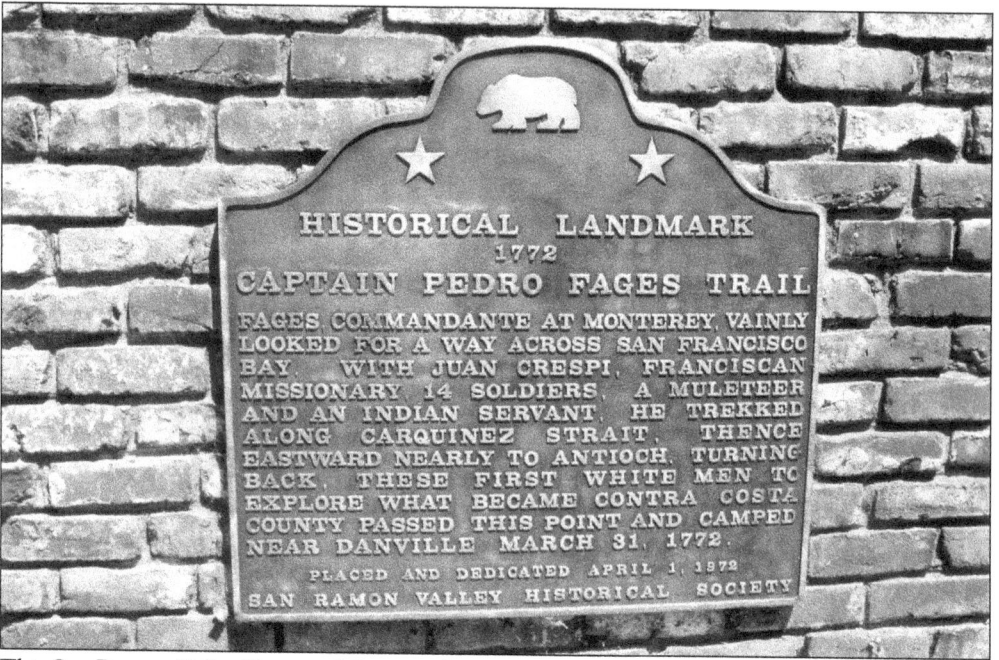

HISTORICAL LANDMARK
1772
CAPTAIN PEDRO FAGES TRAIL

FAGES, COMMANDANTE AT MONTEREY, VAINLY
LOOKED FOR A WAY ACROSS SAN FRANCISCO
BAY. WITH JUAN CRESPI, FRANCISCAN
MISSIONARY, 14 SOLDIERS, A MULETEER
AND AN INDIAN SERVANT, HE TREKKED
ALONG CARQUINEZ STRAIT, THENCE
EASTWARD NEARLY TO ANTIOCH, TURNING
BACK. THESE FIRST WHITE MEN TO
EXPLORE WHAT BECAME CONTRA COSTA
COUNTY PASSED THIS POINT AND CAMPED
NEAR DANVILLE MARCH 31, 1772.

PLACED AND DEDICATED APRIL 1, 1972
SAN RAMON VALLEY HISTORICAL SOCIETY

This San Ramon Valley Historical Society plaque is located at the corner of El Portal and Danville Boulevard. In early 1772, a Spanish expedition led by Capt. Pedro Fages and accompanied by Franciscan missionary Juan Crespi traveled through the East Bay. They were the first westerners seen by local Indians. Father Crespi wrote that the valley had a large variety of trees, fertile land, plenty of water, and "numerous villages of very gentle and peaceful heathen."

Mortars and pestles were important tools for the first people who processed acorns and seeds for daily consumption. Smaller mortars were used to produce paints for face decorations and to grind herbs for special teas. The Museum of the San Ramon Valley features mortars and pestles of several sizes, all found in the San Ramon Valley.

The Franciscan missionaries believed that "they were preparing an impoverished people to live in a glorious afterworld," according to Randall Milliken. In 1797, Mission San Jose was founded just 13 miles north of Mission Santa Clara because Indian hostility prevented placing the mission in the inner valleys. San Jose became very prosperous and was served by two extraordinary missionaries, Fr. Narciso Duran and Fr. Jose Gonzalez Rubio. (Drawing by Al Greger.)

The large Mission San Jose church was rebuilt and restored in 1985, as shown in a modern photograph. The mission's grazing land extended throughout the East Bay's inner valleys. An Indian named Ramon tended cattle and sheep in the San Ramon Valley during winter months. His name was given to the creek and the valley with "San" added to conform to the Spanish usage of the day.

Ranchos were in place for only 15 years, from the mid-1830s until California statehood in 1850. People often romanticized the ranchos. For example, Guadalupe Vallejo wrote, "there never was a more peaceful or happy people on the face of the earth than the Spanish, Mexican, and Indian population of Alta California before the American conquest." (Drawing by Al Greger.)

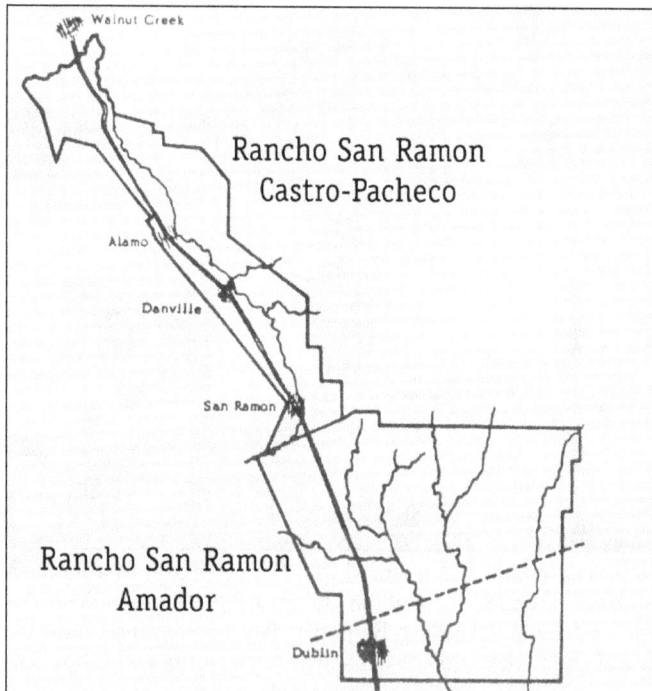

After Mexico became independent, mission lands were granted to Californios, native-born former Spanish soldiers. In 1833, the northern part of the San Ramon Valley was granted to Mariano Castro and his uncle Bartolome Pacheco and became San Ramon Rancho (sometimes with the word Valley affixed). It included over 8,000 acres. South of today's Crow Canyon Road, Jose Maria Amador was granted around 16,500 acres for his San Ramon Rancho in 1834.

Jose Maria Amador was born in 1794 at Mission Dolores, the son of Pedro and Maria Amador. He became a soldier in 1810 and was the civilian administrator at Mission San Jose. Married three times, he had over 20 children. In 1877, he told his story to a writer for H. H. Bancroft; these *Recollections* provide illuminating vignettes of the valley in rancho times.

Amador moved to his rancho in 1826 where he built several two-story adobes at his headquarters (in today's Dublin). At its peak, the rancho's 150 workers produced leather goods, cloth, ranch equipment, and other products. He ran as many as 400 horses and 14,000 cattle and planted vineyards, orchards, and vegetable gardens. He had regular customers to whom he sold his hides, transporting them over the pass (today's I-580) to the bay. (Drawing by John S. Hamel.)

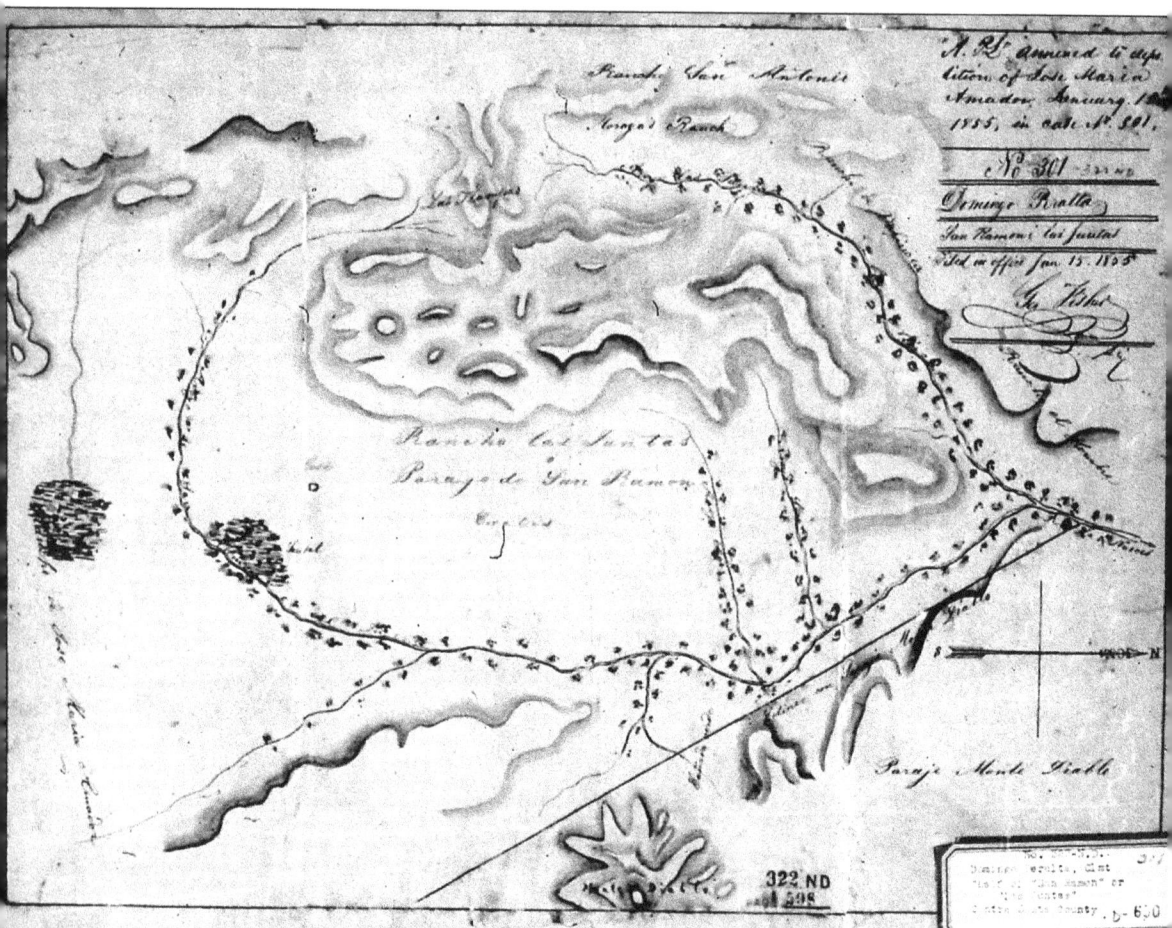

This hand-drawn map (*diseño*) shows the Castro-Pacheco Rancho San Ramon Valley, with north to the right. It is a shortened map of the valley, which extends from today's Crow Canyon Road to Walnut Creek. Notice the large curve, which leads from the top (west) then turns through the drawing's center. This represents San Ramon Creek as it flows out of Bollinger Canyon. Las Trampas hills and Mount Diablo are indicated as are Sycamore Valley and Green Valley creeks. The northern boundary shows the joining of Las Trampas and San Ramon creeks. The original is in color, with green trees lining the creeks.

Three

GOLD RUSH PIONEERS

The San Ramon Valley, west of Mount Diablo, lay at our feet, the richest and most lovely I have yet seen in the state. It is all held in farms, where wheat is grown, and crops of over sixty bushels per acre are expected—such crops does this state produce!

—William H. Brewer, *Up and Down California in 1860–1864*

This gathering at Cox's Grove around 1891 brought families together. Pictured here, from left to right, are (children in first row) Walter Scott, Roger Podva, Roy Halverson, and Robert Podva; (men seated second row) Ed Williams, James Ramage, Charlie Goold, Jim Jones, and Charles Olson; (third row) Jessie Halverson, Mae Halverson (girl), Mrs. Martha Elliot, Mrs. Elizabeth Goold, Mrs. D. P. Williams, Rhoda Maxcy, Lizzie Williams, Fanny Coats Williams, Levi Maxcy, Lizzie Elliot, Evelyn Simpson, Allie Goold Johnson, Hattie Scott, Mrs. Clara Stevens, and Evora Peterson. After the gold rush, new immigrants to California used their earnings from the gold mines to establish themselves in the fertile San Ramon Valley. Most of the newcomers were farmers or had skills to support a rural economy.

Leo Norris was the earliest known American pioneer to buy land and settle in the San Ramon Valley. In 1850, he and his wife, Jane, purchased about 4,500 acres from Jose Maria Amador in the northwest corner of Amador's gigantic San Ramon Rancho. They and their five children, William, Mary, Annie, Jane, and Emily, came to California from Missouri in 1846, traveling part of the way with the ill-fated Donner Party.

Late in 1850, Norris and carpenter William Lynch built the Norris house, a comfortable two-story home with a veranda upstairs, which was first wood frame house in the valley. The redwood logs were obtained from the hills west of Moraga, whip-sawn by hand and hauled by wagon, through Mission San Jose and Sunol Valley. When the house burned down in 1951, it had been occupied for a century.

William Lynch married Mary Norris in 1853 and together they had seven children, all raised in San Ramon. In 1855, they built a two-story redwood house not far from today's Crow Canyon and San Ramon Valley Boulevard. The house was torn down after Lynch Lane became the modern Crow Canyon Road. Lynch raised livestock and grain on a spread of 400 acres. For a time the community was called Lynchville, which recognized his leadership.

In 1846, Mary Ann (Smith) Jones arrived in California with her husband, John, and their children after a grueling wagon trek. Late in 1851, the family moved to Alamo. They helped start a grammar school, Cumberland Presbyterian Church, and the Union Academy. John M. Jones was the first postmaster in 1852, and was an early member of Alamo Masonic Lodge No. 122. Mary lived to be 93 and wrote rich memoirs of her life.

In the early 1850s, pioneers Robert Baldwin and Mary Cox immigrated to the valley. Baldwin and his friend William Meese began gold mining in 1850 and bought prime valley land with their profits in 1852. Mary and Robert Baldwin were married in 1858 and had six children. Baldwin was an innovative farmer, a trustee of the Presbyterian church and Danville Grammar School, and a charter member of the Grange.

In 1888, the Baldwins built a new house, which was described by the *Contra Costa Gazette*: "R. O. Baldwin has 3 teams daily hauling lumber on the ground preparatory to building a ten thousand dollar house on the modern plan, which will be an ornament to our valley." Their new house and barn were completed before the railroad was built. The headquarters of their ranch was located between the county road and the tracks.

The handsome Young family, from left to right, is Robert, Mary, Sarah (child), Alice, and Albert J. In 1862, his family came to the valley when Albert was 21. Later he and Mary Shuey were married. Both of them were well educated and became teachers, sometimes teaching together. A. J. taught in several of the grammar schools, including San Ramon in 1867 and Danville for 17 years.

The Young house was a Folk Victorian house built in 1885. The Youngs, standing in front from left to right, are Albert, Robert (in buggy), Alice, and Mary. The house was called a "gem of architectural beauty" in the 1882 *History of Contra Costa County*. In 1983, it was restored and used as the model for an adjacent office complex at 911 San Ramon Valley Boulevard in Danville.

Brothers Daniel and Andrew Inman first came to the valley in 1852. Dan was a successful miner and, in 1858, he purchased 400 acres of land around the creek in today's Old Town Danville. On the western part of his property he established the first harness and blacksmith shops, sold land to H. W. Harris for a hotel (the first Danville Hotel), and to Michael Cohen for a store and home. Danville is named for him. In 1860, the first post office was established in the Danville Hotel with Harris as postmaster.

The Mendenhall House, built by pioneer William "Philip" Mendenhall in 1853, still stands in the Sycamore Valley. Mary Allen and Mendenhall were married in Santa Clara in 1847, and had 10 children who lived to adulthood. In the turbulent period of the Mexican-American War, he was part of the Bear Flag rebellion and served in John C. Fremont's California Battalion. In 1869, he bought land and laid out the town of Livermore.

The Harlan house and land are shown in this 1879 lithograph. Called "El Nido," this Gothic Revival house has been a well-known landmark since it was built around 1858. Joel Harlan died in 1875, leaving Minerva to manage the ranch and raise eight children. The house was restored in the 1930s by Harlan descendants, the Geldermanns.

In 1846, Minerva Fowler and Joel Harlan were pioneers who came west to California on a wagon train led by Joel's father. Joel went to gold country in 1848, well before "gold fever" spread across the world. Minerva's granddaughter said Minerva never believed gold would be the legal tender because it was too plentiful. In 1852, the Harlans purchased land from the Amador rancho and built a house, which became a boundary marker between Contra Costa and Alameda Counties. El Nido was their second house.

Glass family members are relaxing in front of their house around 1896. Pictured here, from left to right, are Clifford, David, Livia Cox, Chester, Nellie, Eliza, and Anita. David and Eliza purchased over 700 acres three miles south of San Ramon village in 1859 and built homes on the property. The ranch was called the Lora-Nita Ranch for the two Glass sisters who operated it in the 20th century.

This Italianate Victorian house was built by David and Eliza Glass in 1877 on their San Ramon ranch. The image is taken from an 1879 illustrated history. It was called an "elegant mansion" by one writer. There were seven Glass children when they moved in. The house was moved south and is now part of the Forest Home Farms Historic Park, where it has been restored to become a house museum depicting life in the late 19th century.

David and Eliza (Hall) Glass came early to the valley, arriving in 1850. They opened a store south of Walnut Creek (1852) and planted the first fruit orchards in the valley. A leader in the valley, David Glass supported the establishment of schools and churches and worked to bring the railroad to the valley. He was a trustee for the Danville Presbyterian Church (1875) and helped found the San Ramon Methodist Church in the early 1880s.

In front of the Hartz home at the west end of Prospect Avenue, from left to right, are Hannah, Henry, Matilda, Catherine, and John Hartz. John and Catherine Hartz bought 220 acres west of the village of Danville in 1888, grazed cattle, raised corn and grain, and planted orchards. When they retired from the ranch, they built a house (now 455 Hartz Avenue) downtown and he managed the Grange Hall.

Silas and Susanna (Ward) Stone came across the country from Iowa in 1853 with their son Albert Ward Stone. Usually the trip to California was a young person's search for a new life, so the elder Stones brought a mature leadership to the community. Silas was a trustee for the Union Academy, a private high school in south Alamo. Several other Stone family members bought ranch land amounting to over 1,000 acres, hence the area is known as Stone Valley.

The Stones bought a farm about one and one-half miles east of the village of Alamo and, in 1852, built this two-story home on what became Stone Valley Road. The house had nine rooms and was constructed by the Howard brothers using redwood hauled by oxen from the redwoods west of Moraga. In 1954, it was demolished.

In 1892, the Hall house was built by Myron and Lucy Dornan Hall after their five children—Ida, Benjamin, George, Myron, and Ward—had received college educations. In front, from left to right, are George Elbert, Lucy Hall, Myron D. Hall, and Ward Hall (on horseback) about 1895. The house, named "Shady Nook," had walnut trees lining a driveway to the main highway. In 1909, they celebrated a golden wedding anniversary at the house.

Myron Hall was prominent in early valley history, especially in agricultural pursuits and education. Myron came to Alamo in 1853 with the Albert Stone wagon train. He and his wife, Lucy, purchased 103 acres on both sides of the Danville Highway. He successfully grafted Persian walnut cuttings to native black walnut trees and shared these cuttings generously. When he passed away in 1910, he was lauded as the "Father of the Walnut Industry" in the county.

This map records the final American ownership of land in the original Mexican Rancho San Ramon (Castro-Pacheco). The pioneers named on this map bought grazing rights and improved their ranches well before their titles were verified. For example, James Foster, who was justice of the peace, assessor, and Alamo postmaster, said that he purchased land in 1857, obtaining possession but not title. R. O. Baldwin wrote that in 1852, he and William Meese "bought a squatter's right to 160 acres."

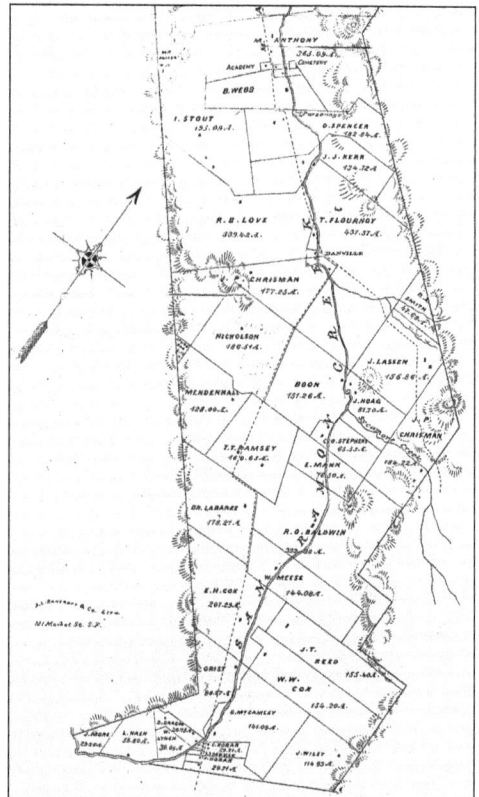

Horace Carpentier, a notorious American land lawyer, got his hands on this property by various types of chicanery and extracted exorbitant amounts of money from the settlers. The title settlement dragged through the courts for years. Many settlers stated that they paid three times over for their land. Imagine the disruption and insecurity this situation caused as pioneers built homes, planted crops, and began families on land with unclear ownership. Finally, in 1865, 65 settlers agreed to pay Carpentier $90,000 in gold coin and received secure titles.

August Hemme was a German immigrant who came to New York in 1846 and to California in 1849. Three years later, he purchased 3,000 acres of fertile land in south Alamo and, in 1856, married neighbor Minerva Ish. An ambitious, energetic, and public spirited man, he left his mark on the valley. In 1890, his leadership was pivotal in persuading Southern Pacific to open the San Ramon Branch Line.

In front of their home in Tassajara are Lawrence family members. Pictured here in 1889, from left to right, are Mariana, Will, Manuel, Joe, George, Nellie, Annie, Josie, Rose, and Belle. The Lawrences were the first Portuguese to immigrate to the valley. Lawrence Road marks the location of their ranch.

In 1865, the Wiedemann house was built in the hills west of San Ramon. Pictured, from left to right, are Christian Wiedemann and his children Mary, Henry, Rose, and Fred. A ship's carpenter from Germany, Christian arrived in 1853, worked in a dairy south of San Francisco, and bought land in San Ramon's brush country with several partners in the 1860s. He married Caterina Dittmer. The Wiedemanns raised cattle, apples, and hay on 480 acres.

Four

VILLAGES IN THE VALLEY

When we reached Alamo, my husband (John Jones) stopped the oxen and said, "Mary, look! Did you ever see anything so beautiful?" There was nothing in sight but Nature . . . After we had looked and talked about it for a while, my husband said, "If I live and can get a home here, I am going to have it." And he never forgot it!

—Virgie V. Jones, *Remembering Alamo*, 1975

The San Ramon Valley Bank served the entire valley and had branches in Danville and Walnut Creek. Standing in front, from left to right, are Herbert Daley, Joe Foster, and Frank Marshall. The villages of Alamo, Danville, and San Ramon provided most businesses needed by the farmers. Pioneer names are recalled on streets and housing developments throughout the valley. Schools such as Rancho Romero, Baldwin, Stone Valley, Charlotte Wood, and Dougherty reflect valley history as well.

In 1911, Henry C. Hurst stands in front of his San Ramon General Merchandise store. Beginning in 1880, his store offered nearly everything rural patrons needed—from clothing to tools to groceries. Hurst was postmaster from 1884 to 1915 and served as Wells Fargo agent from 1887 to 1891. His son Harry was postmaster from 1915 to 1924. People came for their mail and enjoyed a chance to visit with their neighbors.

In 1924, the San Ramon general store was sold to William C. Fereira, who served as postmaster from 1929 to 1963. Pictured in front are his sons, Bill and Cliff, in 1927. Notice the gasoline pumps, constructed in 1926 to keep up with the times. For the many bachelors in the area, this store was a happy gathering place for storytelling and card playing long into the night.

Peter Thorup stands in front of the Thorup Shoe Store in San Ramon, which he opened in 1875 and operated for 55 years—an institution in the small community and valley where practically no one bought ready-made shoes. Thorup Lane, just north of Crow Canyon Road, is named for the family.

Inside the Thorup store, about 1,000 shoe lasts were kept, from which Peter Thorup could custom-make shoes and boots for his many customers. According to the *Contra Costa Gazette* in 1880, Thorup had a successful business, which "keeps two men constantly at work." He married Anne Rasmussen in 1885 and together they welcomed many other Danish immigrants to California. At their 50th anniversary, hundreds came to congratulate them.

In the mid-1880s, the San Ramon Methodist Church was built not far from the schoolhouse. George McCamley and David Glass were involved in founding the church. The first recorded wedding joined Frank Glass and Livia Cox in 1887. The last wedding at the church was that of Claude Glass and Addie Oswill in 1910.

San Ramon was a small town that changed very little over the years. Here is the schoolhouse, general store, blacksmith, and hall around 1950 at the intersection of today's Deerwood Road and San Ramon Valley Boulevard. In 1880, according to the *Contra Costa Gazette*, the village included a hotel, three saloons, two country stores, Thorup's shoe shop, Chinese washhouse, Brewen's blacksmith shop, McPheters' blacksmith, paint, and wheelwright shop, and the schoolhouse.

Front Street was Danville's main street in this c. 1910 view, which includes horses and cars. Shown, from left to right, are the original Cohen's Store, Prospect Avenue, Gibbon's Harness Shop, the Joe McCeil Barber Shop, Conway Store, post office, blacksmith shop, and the Close Store. The post office had a small library upstairs tended by Lillian Close, and the Close Store's upstairs was the meeting room for the Odd Fellows until 1913, when they moved into the new Social and Fraternal Hall.

The San Ramon Hall was built in 1911 in a New England frame style. It provided a much needed and popular location for dances, graduations, meetings, May Day celebrations, and Christmas parties. Minnie C. Lynch and the San Ramon Ladies Association helped raise funds to build the hall. It was an important part of the community for over 50 years.

Volunteers fought fires with water-filled milk cans and gunnysacks in the early years. The Danville Volunteer Fire Department was organized in 1912 with Joe Freitas as chief. In 1921, the Danville Fire Protection District was established which included the Alamo, Danville, Green Valley, and Sycamore School districts. The first elected commission was W. A. Ward, James Jones, and Joe Freitas, who chose Oscar Olsson as the first fire chief. In 1925, this firehouse was built.

Around 1930, these Danville volunteer firefighters are lined up in front of an Autocar Pumper and the firehouse. Pictured, from left to right, are Bill Tarpley, Harold Root, A. M. Fichtenmueller, Steve Johnson, George Todoroff, Alfred Cabral, Jim Dondero, Bert Read, Pete Lynch, Austin Root, Tony Cabral, George Wood, Jim Root, unidentified, and Duane Elliott. The siren, in back of the firehouse, was activated by the telephone operator across the street.

The classic New England–style Danville Presbyterian Church was called by one writer, "the handsomest church in the County." Dedicated in 1876, an unusual vote of all community Protestants (Congregationalists, Methodists, Presbyterians, and Christians) decided to build a Presbyterian church. The first minister Rev. R. S. Symington is featured in this picture. J. J. Kerr, Robert O. Baldwin, and David Glass were the first trustees. It burned down in 1932 and was replaced by a Mission-style church, which is now the Town Meeting Hall.

SAINT ISIDORE'S CHURCH DANVILLE CAL.

When a new Danville Catholic parish was established in 1910, the first St. Isidore's Catholic Church was located at the southeast corner of Hartz Avenue and Linda Mesa. Before the church and rectory were ready, mass was said in the Danville Grange Hall, and Rev. Fr. John Collins lived at the Danville Hotel. In 1911, Council No. 3 of the Danville UPEC (a Portuguese fraternal lodge) donated the original bell to the church. In 1963, the original St. Isidore's was razed.

47

Halverson's Livery Stable was built on a large lot on Hartz Avenue—after the railroad came to Danville in 1891. John Halverson and his son Roy ran the stable, which provided riding horses, single and double teams, and boarding for local residents' horses. Salesmen who arrived by train could rent a horse and buggy for $1.50 or a surrey with two horses for $3. The Halversons planted redwood trees, which can still be seen today.

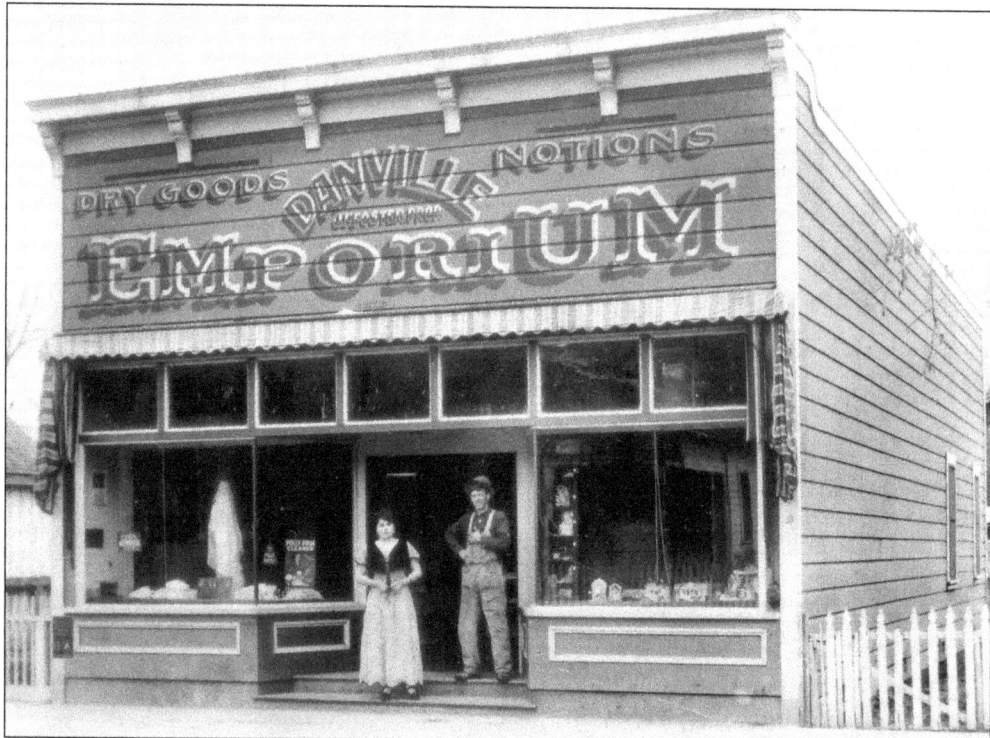

Joseph Foster and his first wife, Elizabeth, stand in front of the Danville Emporium in early 1914. It was a general store with a wide range of merchandise such as needles, thread, fabric, dolls, greeting cards, and clothing. The Danville Emporium and three adjacent houses burned down in 1926 after Annie Foster's jelly spilled over and started a fast-moving kitchen fire. She snatched up baby Josephine and barely escaped.

Hiram and Tillie (Hartz) Elliott stand holding son Duane in front of their new Craftsman-style house on Diablo Road in 1910. Hiram was a jockey who learned the hotel bar business. He ran the Lawless Saloon at Front and Diablo for owner Charles Gust, then purchased and renamed it in 1907. In 1912, the bar was moved to its present location on Hartz Avenue.

This view of Elliott's shows George Groom on the far right. The bar was owned and operated by Hiram Elliott and his sons, Duane and Gordon, for 70 years. In 1925, the first fire station was built directly across from Elliott's. The bar was a favorite spot for volunteer firemen who, of course, could not predict when a fire would occur. In the 1920s, Elliott's became the Danville Ice Cream Parlor since Hiram refused to break Prohibition law and sell liquor out the back door.

49

In 1922, McDonald's drugstore was built in a Spanish eclectic style, for a cost of $10,000. This building still stands at 345 Hartz Avenue. The first floor was a drugstore with an ice cream fountain and news depot. The family lived upstairs. Later it was a pharmacy owned by the Rodgers (from 1938 to 1945) and the Randalls (after 1945).

Large water tanks for farm and ranch use were created at A. M. Fichtenmueller's shop on the northwest corner of Front Street and Diablo. Joe Foster and Fichtenmueller stand in front of the tank, which was east of Olsson's Garage. Fichtenmueller was active in the fire department, serving as a volunteer fireman, captain, commissioner, and chief.

The Vecki family poses in front of their Gothic Revival house, built by the Howard Brothers in 1866 for Michael Cohen on Front Street. The Veckis arrived in Danville after the San Francisco earthquake and purchased the house in 1906. Dr. Vecki practiced dentistry there. Pictured here, from left to right, are Mary N. Allen (Claire Vecki's mother), Claire, Victor, Victor Jan, and Isabel.

The first Danville Hotel, built in 1858, burned down in 1873. Pictured here is the "new" Danville Hotel built after the railroad came in 1891. Located east of the Danville station on Railroad Avenue, the McCauley family owned and ran the 8- to 10-room hotel. Salesmen from the train and bachelor workers stayed there. The hotel and McCauley residence were moved to face Hartz Avenue in 1927, where they remain today.

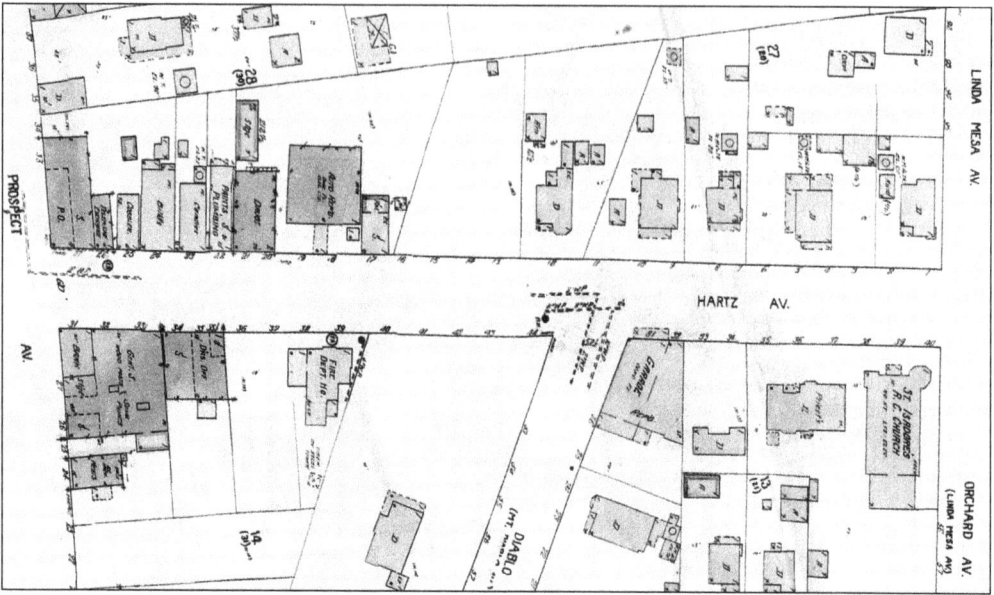

The Sanborn Map Company created insurance maps, which described the water supplies, building materials, and fire departments in communities. This map of Danville shows a population of 718. California Water Service Corporation supplied water in a 10-inch main and the fire alarm was a siren on a steel tower. The post office and bank are on the left and St. Isidore's church is on the right in this 1932 map.

The San Ramon Valley Bank's Danville Branch was erected at a cost of $15,000 on the corner of North Hartz and East Prospect Avenues by 1911. Danville Branch manager was local businessman Clarence W. Close; presidents included R. O. Baldwin in 1911 and Numa S. Boone in 1916. In 1931, it was bought by the Bank of America.

The Danville Machine Works was on the corner of Railroad and today's San Ramon Valley Boulevard at the south end of town. As automobiles became more popular, gas stations and garages were built along State Highway 21, the main road through the valley.

Groom's Blacksmith shop was located at the southeast corner of West Prospect and Railroad Avenues. On the right, about 1920, is Canadian immigrant George Groom. A constable for years, Groom belonged to the Odd Fellows and was the first assistant fire chief when the Danville Volunteer Fire Department was organized in 1912.

The Alamo post office began in 1852 and for years was the only post office between Martinez and San Jose. Bell's store had the post office from 1910 to 1936, at the corner of today's Las Trampas and Danville Boulevard. For a time it was called Bell's Post Office Store. Residents could buy groceries and pick up the mail. Mrs. Bell is pictured out front.

On the front porch of Bell's store, from left to right, are Mr. and Mrs. David Bell and children Harriett, Mary, Alice, Ora, and Bertha. This store was an important fixture in Alamo. The Bells served as postmasters for over 50 years: David Bell (1905–1923), Roy Bell (1923–1936), Harriet Bell Hunt (1936–1944), and Bertha Bell Linhares (1947–1960).

In 1894, this Victorian house was built by August and Annie (Stone) Humburg at 24 Orchard Court, Alamo, shortly after their wedding. It was built of redwood and cedar with the living areas on the upper level. Both August and Annie were born in Alamo to pioneer parents—the Humburgs from Germany and the Stones from Iowa. Pictured, from left to right, are daughter Friederiche and Annie Stone Humburg holding baby Lorenz.

The Alamo post office was in several locations, including an adobe building, the Henry Hotel, and Bell's Store. In 1936, postmaster Harriet Bell Hunt built a small building dedicated to post office in front of her home, located to the south of Las Trampas Road. In the 1940s, the building was moved north and, in 2005, is a shoe repair shop.

Built by the Howard brothers in 1858, the Henry Hotel was named for one of the owners, Henry Hoffman. An important Alamo landmark for nearly 100 years, it was a boarding house, held the post office for a time, and was dismantled in 1954 when a gas station was built in its place.

The Alamo Cemetery began on a gentle hill east of San Ramon Creek during the 1850s. Cemetery plots include many San Ramon Valley pioneer families. The main path includes Podva, Stow, Stone, Noia, and Boone family members. A public nondenominational cemetery and special district, its park-like setting and many pioneer graves make the cemetery a favorite visitor destination. (Drawing by Paul Dunlap.)

In 1912, charismatic entrepreneur Robert Noble Burgess purchased Oakwood Park Stock Farm and transformed it into a swank summer resort, one of the first California country clubs. He envisioned a modern scenic boulevard leading to Mount Diablo's summit, an elaborate mountain hotel and tower, and the Mount Diablo Park Club. The club eventually included an inn, golf course, tennis courts, horse stables, and beach recreation at Diablo Lake. Promotional parties drew visitors from far and wide.

In 1917, the Diablo Chalet building was built for Mount Diablo Park Club members and guests. Architect Arthur Benton created a 39-room chalet, including suites of different sizes, which sold for $2,830 and more. Initially the chalet was connected to the inn by a covered bridge over the creek. Remodeled in the 1970s, the chalet consists of eight modern condominium units and is part of the Diablo Country Club.

The 1889 Tassajara schoolhouse (shown in 1912) looks very similar to the schoolhouse today, with its bell tower, front steps, walnut trees, and stable. Children whose parents came from different countries and back east learned to be Californians together. Students still recall satisfying lunch exchanges—Portuguese linguisa and sweet bread for Danish egg salad sandwiches slathered with butter.

The Tassajara post office on Finley Road, shown here with the mail slot in front, was opened so residents would not have to go into Pleasanton or Danville for their mail. This board and batten utility shed, adjacent to an elegant farmhouse built years before by John Wilkes, became the first post office on October 24, 1896, with George Cole as postmaster. It closed in 1922.

Five

HORSE COUNTRY

Prize cattle and horse shows were held and cattlemen from all over the world came to the Blackhawk.

—Centennial Edition, *Contra Costa Gazette*, September 18, 1958

The distinctive architecture and dimensions of the Oakwood Park Stock Farm carriage barn reflect the size and quality of this ranch. From 1890 to 1912, John and Louise Boyd created an outstanding horse and cattle breeding farm at Oakwood. Further east, Blackhawk Ranch bred Shire horses, and the Johnston Ranch in Tassajara was known for its Clydesdale and Norman purebred horses. Every part of life, from transport to farm work, depended on horses.

Nestled south of Mount Diablo, the farm included 6,000 acres in 1895, with 2,500 acres cultivated in crops such as hay, wheat, barley, alfalfa, and fruit. A large reservoir upland from Oakwood Farm held 30 million gallons and supplied ample water.

The Oakwood Farm barns and stable complex were extensive. An article on the farm states: "The best proof of the adaptability of Oakwood Park for stock breeding is the appearance of the horses and cattle. Some seven hundred or more in these two departments, old and young, with few exceptions, hearty and strong."

In 1868, a wagon from the Norris Ranch is loaded with sacks of grain pulled by a six-mule team. Wheat and other grains were transported on freight wagons to wharves in Pacheco and Martinez. Horses were essential to early cultivated agriculture and were used to power agricultural equipment and transport goods and people.

Mark Elliot was an early pioneer in the valley, who arrived in 1852, built a house in 1858, and ranched in the Tassajara Valley. A cabinet-maker by trade, Elliot came to California from Ohio during the gold rush and manufactured rockers for gold miners, an occupation which was far steadier than panning for gold.

Stable hands took excellent care of the valuable Oakwood horses. Here Muriel Wiley is shown off. One famous horse, Steinway, was purchased in 1879 for $17,000. The *Contra Costa News* wrote on July 1, 1897, "This is the home of the celebrated trotting stallion, Steinway, known to every horseman in America."

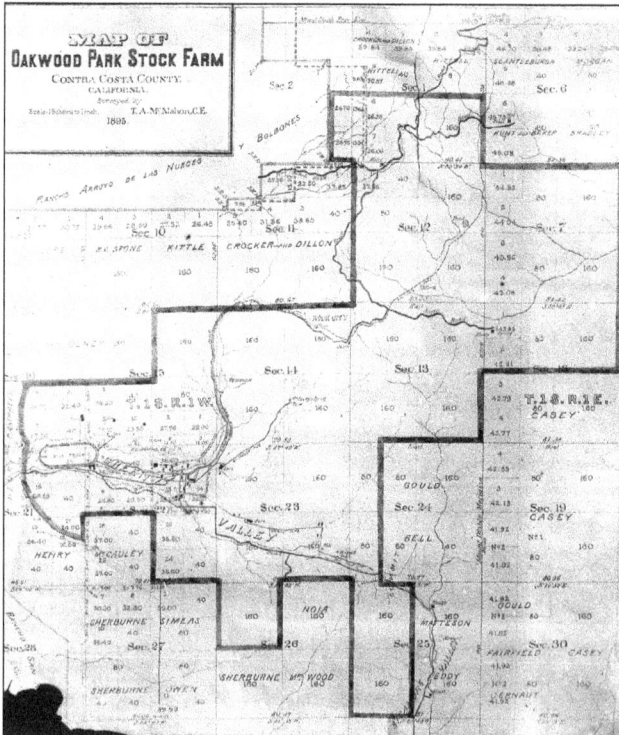

This map of Oakwood shows the size of the ranch, which extended far up Mount Diablo. The training track is observed at the lower left, not far from Diablo Road and Green Valley Creek. The *Contra Costa News* proclaimed, "Nowhere in California or perhaps in the world is there a spot so admirably adapted to the purpose of stock-raising as the little valley setting off from the San Ramon and occupied by the Oakwood Park Stock Farm."

Contra Costa pioneers loved harness races. There were tracks in Concord, Walnut Creek, and Oakwood Farm. One of their horses, Oakwood, is shown here winning the Decoration Day race in Pleasanton on May 30, 1912, in a one-mile time of 2 minutes, 16 seconds. This horse was owned by Danville blacksmith A. J. Abrott.

The training track at Oakwood is touted in a brochure as "first class," with its springy surface, ornamental plantings, and fruit, olive, and almond trees. It states that "the object was to make it a counterpart of the best public race courses." Eucalyptus trees, which bordered the track, can still be seen at Diablo Country Club.

August Humburg raced his horse Humburg Belle at the Oakwood track. This buggy (with the Humburg house in the background) shows the typical way people traveled in the 19th century. August's father, Friederick, emigrated from Germany to California at age 26 to work in the gold mines. In 1853, he moved to Alamo, married Maria Kornman (1863), and resumed his trade of making harnesses.

Meat was delivered throughout the valley in this Danville Market wagon, pulled by a gentle horse and driven by the jaunty Joseph E. Lawrence. His father, Joseph C. Lawrence, opened a butcher shop on Prospect Avenue in Danville in 1897 where he sold meat, poultry, milk, cream, and eggs from local ranches. Louis Pelligrini, whose friendliness and fondness for singing opera were recalled by many, delivered fresh fish by horse and cart as well. His nickname was "Louie the Fish Man."

Blackhawk Ranch was famous for its prize Shire horses. According to a 1958 *Contra Costa Gazette* history article: "Winning top honors at the American, International and Shows everywhere, Easton & Ward took more first prizes than any breeder had ever won in a single year." After 1934, when Raymond C. Force bought the ranch and increased the acreage to 6,500 acres, he raised prize Arabian horses and started an extensive Hereford cattle operation.

Blackhawk Ranch was established east of Danville in 1917, when Ansel M. Easton and his son-in-law William A. Ward purchased 1,250 acres of hilly terrain south of Mount Diablo. The family built a large showcase house in a small valley, designed by Louis Mulgardt at a cost of $50,000. The barn surrounded a courtyard with lawn, which allowed them to show registered Shire workhorses and pure-bred Shorthorn cattle.

In 1937, Fred Wiedemann rides his horse Gila Bend. Raising cattle on a ranch meant hours of work on horseback. The Wiedemann Ranch grew from an original 480 acres in the 1860s to around 4,500 acres in the 20th century. Annual roundups for branding broke up the work and offered a chance to see friends.

In 1931, 18 horses pulled the Wiedemann's gas engine-powered combine in the Sherburne hills. Dependable tractors able to operate safely on steep hillsides were not yet common, so horses continued to perform certain ranch and farm jobs. This harvester had a self-leveling platform powered by the engine.

This five-horse team pulls a two-bottom plow, used mostly on the flat valley soils. People had to spend time tending their horses. One writer said, "When your only transportation is by the use of horses, there is the care, feeding, watering, currying, brushing and cleaning the barns."

The 1966 Danville Hotel's parade entry commemorates the days when the valley was horse country. Vivian Coats recalled riding horseback to grammar and high school from Tassajara Valley. She and her cousin Undine Horton liked to race the horses in wet weather so they could splash one another with mud. They wore divided riding skirts and changed to dresses left at the Danville High School on Front Street.

A Junior Monarch five-wire dump-off hay press works where the Round Hill Country Club is today. Two horses, running in a circle, powered this machine and were rotated regularly. Horses were replaced after about a half hour and were allowed to eat and rest for a couple of hours before their turn came again. One horse was used to pull the loose hay onto the feeding platform while another brought hay to the press. Baling was done from dawn to dusk.

In this 20th-century photograph, workers load bundled grain onto a wagon. After ripe grain was cut with a binder and bound into bundles, grain was taken to a stationary thresher.

Six

SCHOOL DAYS

In its early days the Sycamore School was a public center for important events—social activities, picnics, parties, school "exhibitions", etc. A literary society, Sunday school and church services conducted at various times and occasionally a Christmas tree celebration were held in this pleasant gathering place.

—Centennial Edition, *The Valley Pioneer*, 1958.

San Ramon Valley Union High School, shown in 1930, began in a Danville house in 1910. Initiated by a Danville Grange committee in 1909, it was the valley's first public high school. Classes also met upstairs in a Front Street store (1914–1917) before moving to the new Mission-style high school north of Danville in 1917. Before the first grammar schools were built, young children were instructed in homes, including those of the Glasses, Bryants, Norrises, Harlans, Howards, and Stones. Simple one-room schools were built, followed by more elaborate ones in Alamo, San Ramon, Danville, Green Valley, Sycamore, and Tassajara.

Twenty-year-old Bret Harte tutored children at the Abner Bryant ranch in Tassajara Valley, near Alamo Creek. In an 1856 letter to his sister, Harte said that Bryant "had four young sons, and not caring to have them grow up like range-cattle, he decided to have a tutor." Harte, author of *A Legend of Monte Diablo* and *First Family of Tasajara*, became one of the West's most famous pioneer writers. He is pictured here in 1878.

EAST ELEVATION   NORTH ELEVATION   1859 · UNION ACADEMY · 1868

San Ramon Valley residents organized a large private high school in 1859, located midway between Alamo and Danville, and led by trustees Silas Stone, John M. Jones, and Robert Love. The Union Academy's modern curriculum included instruction in reading, geography, mathematics, history, foreign languages, and vocal music. It served students who boarded and valley students who lived at home. During the summer of 1868, the schoolhouse burned down. (Drawing by John S. Hamel.)

Students are shown in front of the first public high school, the Eddy House, located on Church Street in Danville. It was rented for $25 a month by the newly elected board of trustees—John F. Baldwin, Will E. Stewart, Charles J. Wood, William Meese, A. H. Cope, and David Bell. In three rooms, six courses, including commercial, history, English, German, mathematics, and physical geography were taught. In 1912, a fourth room was added for a chemistry and physics laboratory.

Five seniors graduated from the San Ramon Valley Union High School on May 29, 1914, the high school's first commencement. It was held in the new Social and Fraternal Hall on Danville's Front Street. The graduates, from left to right, are Astrid Olsson, Ora Bell, Ruth Weinhauser, Viola Lynch, and Alice Bell. Viola Lynch recalled that she and Astrid Olsson rode horseback to the high school from San Ramon.

Late in the summer of 1914, high school classes moved to the renovated Odd Fellows meeting rooms, upstairs in a building owned by the Close family on Front Street. One student wrote that the floor shook if you stomped on it. Students learned surveying in a nearby field.

In 1915, the high school student body poses in front of the school. Pictured, from left to right, are (first row) Maude Donahue, Christine Sorrensen, Christine Rutherford, Florence Pynn, Georgia Burris, and Sophie Sorrensen; (second row) Charles Stelling, Travis Boone, Alton Wilcox, Ruth Crozier, Christine Andreasen, Florence Burris, Ila Boucher, Undine Horton, Geneva Billings, Alberta Wiedemann, Vivian Coats, Bernice Donahue, Catherine Stelling, and Arthur Peters; (third row) Phillip Harris, Leo (Pete) Lynch, Durward Van Gordon, Lloyd Williams, Raymond Andreasen, Milton Smith, David Boucher, Braddock Petersen, Claude Andreasen, Lloyd Abrott, Reuben Olsson, Roy Bell, and Oliver Davis.

In 1921, students are pictured in front of the new high school. The first school board was dedicated to getting the high school in place. They hired teachers, approved curriculum, bought supplies, and, in 1915, purchased 10 acres of land north of Danville from Mr. McAdue, a butcher who used the property as a slaughter yard. Norman R. Coulter, a San Francisco architect, designed the building, which opened in 1917.

During the 1910s, commercial buildings on Front Street in Danville served the farmers and ranchers, providing a general merchandise store, a barber, a blacksmith, and the post office. Notice the Independent Order of Odd Fellows (IOOF) building, which was the upstairs site of the high school. Early school picnics were often held at Ramona Park, the Meese Ranch picnic grounds south of town.

This is the first grammar school in the village of Alamo. Over the years, three Alamo grammar schools were built near today's northwest corner of Stone Valley Road and Danville Boulevard. The 2.5 acre property on which these schools were located was sold for $200 by Mary Ann Jones to be used for school purposes. In 1869, the school had 52 students. The 1873 trustees were J. M. Shuey, J. Thirston, and A. W. Stone. In 1893, this school was destroyed by fire.

In 1900, the Alamo Grammar School students, from left to right, are (first row) ? Mueller, Archie Penfield, George Samuels, Jack Reis, unidentified, and Joe Bispo; (second row) Maggie Olivier, Mary Bispo, Martha Bunce, Mary Nunes, Nina Bell, Grace Samuels, ? Mueller, Mary Bell, and Harriett Bell; (third row) Albert Stone, Belle Nunes, Lilas Stone, ? Mueller, Bertha Stone, ? Mueller, unidentified, and Fred Shoen; (fourth row) Miss Gruenig, Stewart Kennedy, unidentified, Addie Smith, Sadie Smith, Elvira Smith, Olivette Bunce, Gustave Reis, and Ray Grenell.

This well-loved school, the second Alamo Grammar School, was remodeled several times over the years. The original bell tower was removed and the bell placed in the outside yard, presumably because of earthquake safety concerns. In 1904, 61 children were enrolled. Today's Alamo Elementary School at 100 Wilson Road has the original Alamo School bell in its courtyard.

The third Alamo Grammar School was built in 1940 and closed in 1965. Teacher Irene Mlejnik is shown with her students in 1950. Students, from left to right, are (first row) Jimmy Morin, Michael Powell, Michael Mivelaz, Charlie Clark, Guy Wulfing, Steven Niino, Denny Putnam, Ronnie Catania, Tom Crouch, and Bobby Nickerson; (second row) Carla Diehl, Karen Nelson, Sue Henderson, Pattie Briggs, Susan Funk, Leslie Green, Mary Beauchamp, Charlene Havercroft, Enid Santiago, Marilyn Sherk, Cindy Gartin, Marjorie Moore, Sheryl Hendricks, Judith Romley, and Mary Overcast.

While the first Danville Grammar School was built south of town in 1858, later ones were placed near Front Street. In early 1867, the *Contra Costa Gazette* wrote: "A social reunion is to be given at the new School House near Danville . . . Good music, good company and a good time may be anticipated." A. J. Young, who taught Danville students from 1883 to 1900, stands with his students. R. O. Baldwin, James O. Boone, and Jonathan Hoag were the first trustees.

Students in front of the Danville school *c.* 1894, from left to right, are (first row) Joe Cabral, ? Ramage, ? Ramage, A. Kushing, Tony Cabral, ? Keesling, Sarah Young, ? Olivera, Esma Boone, unidentified, and ? Silva; (second row) Herb Shuey, Ed Hampton, John Chrisman, Ethel Chrisman, Mabel Hoag, ? Silva, unidentified, unidentified, Marcus Donlan, and ? Silva; (third row) Roy Halverson, Susie Boone, Mabel Simpson, Marie Burgess, Bill Hemme, Mae Halverson, and Clarence Shuey; (fourth row) Armstrong Stewart, A. J. Young (teacher), Julian Thompson, F. Peters, Robert Hoag, Nellie McParker, Jesse Hoag, Matilda Hartz Elliott, Bob Burgess, ? Silva, Clem Close, Alice Hampton, Ted Thompson, F. Cabral, and ? Silva.

In 1896, Danville residents proudly dedicated a new schoolhouse with a bell tower. After a $5,000 bond had been passed for a new school, the *Contra Costa Gazette* article in 1895 stated "We . . . want our school house to be one of the most prominent buildings in the valley, located on such a street and facing in a direction to attract attention from any transient traveler or tourist through our valley. Let everybody know we have an interest in education by looking at the building."

In 1904, 80 students attended the Danville school. When Hazel Arthur (Wiester) taught in 1911, there were eight grades with 64 children. By that time, state law required two teachers for that number of students, so she taught grades five through eight and Maryann Burell taught grades one through four. A huge potbelly stove sat in the middle of the room. Mrs. Wiester recalled a good-sized library and an organ.

Danville Grammar School 1949
Photo by Davies Alamo, Cal.

The last Danville Grammar School was built in 1922 at Love Lane, in a modern style. It opened in January 1923. Margaret Baldwin remembered carrying her books from the school on Front Street to the new one when she was in fourth grade. Later Green Valley, Sycamore, and Tassajara Grammar schools closed and students came to this school, as their school populations shrank and parents thought the Danville school offered other advantages.

The only 19th-century, one-room schoolhouse still standing is the Tassajara School House at 1650 Finley Road. This was the second Tassajara grammar school. All 10 voters approved the sale of school bonds for $1,700 and Peter Anderson sold an acre of his land for the school. When he attended in the 1890s, Roger Podva recalled 40 to 75 students at the school, sitting two to a desk. Podva said the school's black walnut trees were planted by the children.

The class of 1887 is near the first Tassajara School House. Pictured, from left to right, are (first row) Frank Davina, Chester Johnston, Tony Olivera, Manuel Antone, John Kroeger, John Madeiros, Willie Hanna, Charlie Hanna, and Alfred Podva; (second row) Elsie McPherson, Louise Finley, Jennie Coats, Abbie Finley, May Coats, Mary Davina, Agusta Koch, Lucy Finley, and Ella Fergoda; (third row) Mamie Fergoda, Lizzie Koch, Wilson Finley, Ella Coats, Ernest McPherson, Nina McPherson, Richard Williams (teacher), Ella Drennan, Ed Williams, Phoebe Bowles, Mary Finley, Clarence McPherson, Bertha Hanna, and Rose Davina.

By 1946, there were only 16 students at the Tassajara Grammar School and the school closed. The students in the final class, from left to right, are (first row) James Faria, Gordon Rasmussen, and Arnold Caldeira; (second row) Eddie Faria, Janet Reinstein, Kristine Nielsen, Laura Ann Reinstein, Elaine Bettencourt, Pete Reinstein, and Nancy Rasmussen; (third row) Betty Mattos, Antoinette Faria, Richard Bettencourt, Eugene Caldeira, Patty Newman, Catherine Newman, and Mrs. Gertrude Arendt, the teacher.

The San Ramon Grammar School, an all-wood structure, had two rooms with 13-foot ceilings and a bell tower. Teacher Mary Wilson stands in front with her students. In 1867, carpenter Ebenizer Dole built the 46-foot by 26-foot school. According to the *Contra Costa Gazette* in 1874, "the building is one among the neatest and best arranged school houses in the county." The San Ramon Methodist Church can be seen in the background.

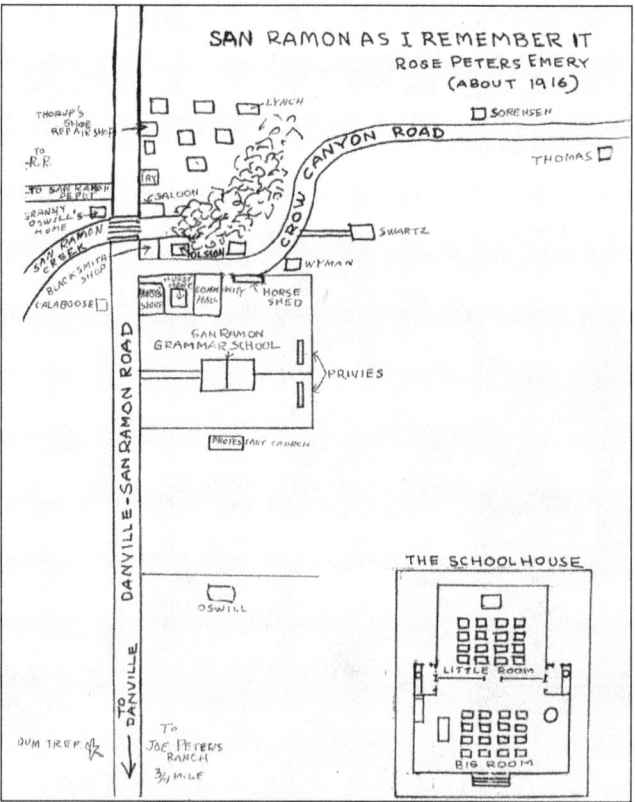

This c. 1916 drawing of San Ramon was done by Rose Peters Emery. It outlines the schoolhouse rooms partitioned in the middle. Howard Wiedemann and Leo Lynch recalled removing the room's central partition for dancing. Meetings, parties, and dances were held there regularly until the larger San Ramon Hall was built in 1911.

The first San Ramon school was located north of the village in 1852. By 1866, San Ramon voters supported a $2,000 bond issue for a new schoolhouse in town. In 1869, 68 students were enrolled at the school. This school is affectionately remembered by its students, who attended until it closed in 1951.

In 1914, the entire San Ramon Grammar School student body had its picture taken. Teachers are Ella Boucher, left, and Blanche Wilson, right. Students, from left to right, are (first row) Rose Peters, Less Thomas, Petrea Thorup, Mary Souves, Thelma Oswill, Varonica Cabral, Evelyn Peters, and Vita Jensen; (second row) Helen Read, Dorothy Wilcox, Josh Souves, Loury Loston, Tony Souves, Antonio Santas, Simson Johnson, Ken Fry, Tony Fernandos, Polly Fereira, Tony Gonzalves, E. Gonsalves, Leonora Santas, Mary Mattos, and Amelie Santos; (third row) Joe Mattos, ? Souves, Bert Peters, Ed Olsson, Rowland Gass, Ed Peters, Ambrose Swartz, M. Santas, Manuel Mattos, Eleanor Boone, Ramona Read, Christ Sorenson, Travis Boone, Joe Rosaf, and Ed Fereira.

Pictured here is Charlotte E. Wood, Sycamore Grammar School student from 1869 to 1877 and Sycamore Grammar School teacher from 1890 to 1921.

This rare indoor school picture shows desks, a blackboard, and a potbelly stove. According to Charlotte E. Wood, some of the text books of the 1870s and 1880s were *Robinson's Practical Arithmetic*, *Swinton's Word Book*, *Reed and Kellogg's Grammar*, and *Willson's* and *McGuffey's Readers*.

The Sycamore Grammar School was organized in 1865 and built by Ebenizer Dole in 1866 on land donated by pioneer Wade Hays. Miss Mary Hall taught 17 students that year. The first trustees were Charles Wood, William Simpson, and Wade Hayes. Pictured at the door is longtime teacher Charlotte E. Wood and two students. Until 1927, this schoolhouse served Sycamore Valley students.

Sycamore Valley students and teacher Kate Howard are pictured in 1889, from left to right, (first row) Willie Lawrence, Joe Lawrence, Manuel Lawrence, Oscar Harris, Claude Harris, and unidentified; (second row) ? Leandro, Mariana Leandro, unidentified, unidentified, Isabel Lawrence, Mariana Lawrence, Ella Grosser, unidentified, and ? Leandro; (third row) Julia Juylo, Mary Juylo, Rose Lawrence, John Ferrera, Charlie Scott, Teacher Kate Howard, Nellie Lawrence, Agnes Grosser, Julie Leandro, Edgar Harris, Josie Lawrence, and Hattie Scott.

Proud students are in front of Green Valley School with teacher Mrs. Mills. Pictured here, from left to right, are (first row) Lois Johnson, Emma Cuneo, Tillie Peterson, Andrew Anderson, Ralph Short, Will Donahue, and Joe Cuneo; (second row) Matilda Jorgensen, Grace Donahue, Louise Noia, Maude Donahue, Isabel Noia, Fred Noia, Paul Noia, and Elmer Short. The 11 Noia children lived about two miles east of the school. The school bell, engraved "1867," is now at Green Valley Elementary School, which was built in 1952.

The first Green Valley Grammar School was designed by Nathanial Howard on land donated by Andrew Inman. In 1865, neighbors built the school on a hill on the northwest corner of today's Green Valley and Blemer Roads for $575. In 1866, enrollment was 24 students. Pictured on the school knoll, from left to right, are two unidentified students, Lois Johnson, Matilda Jorgensen, Emma Cuneo, Louise Noia, Joe Cuneo, Mrs. Mills, Andy Anderson, Isabel Noia, unidentified, Tillie Peterson, Fred Noia, Maude Donahue, and Paul Noia.

Seven

RED-LETTER DAYS

What is probably the oldest continuous series of dances in Contra Costa county is conducted monthly in the Danville veterans' hall by the Mt. Diablo post of the American Legion. On the first Saturday night of each month the post and women's auxiliary have an oldtime dance where middle-aged folk may enjoy the polka, schottische, mazurka, Danish polka, Tye waltz, two-step, quadrille, lancers and other dances they learned when children.

—*Walnut Kernel Special, 1941*

In 1895, family and friends met at the Woodside Farm in Sycamore Valley. From left to right, they are (first row) Charles Wood, Kate Howard, unidentified, Mary Fairfield, Lizzie Elliot, and David Caldwell; (second row) Jennie Baldwin, Charlotte (Lottie) Wood, Mrs. Charles (Cynthia) Wood, Ida S. Hall, Mira More, and Jessie Cox; (third row) June Root, James Jones, Charles J. Wood, John Wood, Fred B. More, Elmer Baldwin, Joseph A. White, and Elizabeth (Libbie) Wood. Picnics, May Day and Fourth of July celebrations, trips to Mount Diablo, and parades punctuated the hard everyday life of the valley's farm and ranch families.

Festive groups stayed on Mount Diablo and dubbed their sites names like Camp Humbug and Camp Jolly. A *Semi-Weekly Gazette* article in 1889 said Camp Jolly had a "brass band, a choral society and a gun club." The group cooked venison, fended off some rattlesnakes, and hiked to the eastern summit, beginning at 4:00 a.m. and returning at 8:30 p.m.

In 1897, this group of friends from the Tasssajara Valley went to Yosemite. It took three days to reach the valley where they could view Yosemite Falls and camp by the Merced River. From left to right, they are Lena Prindle, Eunice and Doris Coats, little Bethel and Phoebe Coats.

In 1906, the Meese family opened a 10-acre group picnic site on their ranch next to the Southern Pacific Railroad line. Ramona Park was located west of the Iron Horse Regional Trail near today's Greenbrook Drive. Because of the San Francisco earthquake on April 18, the park opening was moved to July 4. That day 25 percent of the receipts were turned over to the earthquake relief committee. The program was planned by Danville Lodge No. 378 of the Independent Order of Odd Fellows.

OPENING

OF

RAMONA PARK

Thursday, April 26

COME AND ENJOY YOURSELF

The *Martinez Daily Gazette* in 1906 assured readers that Ramona Park "will undoubtedly be recognized in a short while as the first of California's many parks for pleasure seekers." Run on temperance principles, the park included large shade trees, a dance pavilion, and a lake. The day it opened, a special train left San Francisco at 8:00 a.m., stopped at intervening stations, and returned from the park at 5:00 p.m.

Around 1890, this group picnicked under the trees at Cox's Grove, which was located north of San Ramon. The adults, from left to right, are (first row) Ella Peterson, Ella Coats, Loreta Glass, James Coats, Minnie Harlan, Mabel Harlan, and Carrie Ledden; (second row), Ida Hall, unidentified, unidentified, Elisha Harlan, Mira More, Laura More, Lilly Glass, Albert Glass), Kate Howard, Jennie Baldwin, Helena Hemme, Ed Shuey, Lillie Elliott, Mary More, Samuel Ramage, and Jim Ramage. No children are identified.

Pioneers, gathered at Cox's Grove c. 1890, stopped for a picture. They are, from left to right, Albert W. Glass, Joe Lewis (?), Milton Larabee, William Meese, Levi Maxcy, Edward McCauley, Samuel Ramage, Lee Parker (?), Edward Shuey, Albert W. Stone, Samuel More, Charles G. Goold, John P. Chrisman, Myron W. Hall, David Glass, William Z. Stone, Nathaniel Howard, Robert O. Baldwin, James O. Boone, William Cox, George McCamley, and Elisha C. Harlan. Ida Hall provided these names.

In 1914, "Uncle Sam" appeared in one of the parties at Woodside Farm in the person of Howard Wood. As Charlotte Wood wrote, "Scores of Red Letter Days have left indelible memories scattered lovingly and unsparingly along the Woodside pathway, for the Wood Clan were always prone to celebrate in some fitting manner any event of note, the arrival of an Eastern Guest, a wedding anniversary or birthday."

A gala group in 1906 posed for the camera in Tassajara. From left to right are (first row) Meta Alberg Daltan, child Alberg Dalton, and Bert Dalton; (second row) Phoebe Short, Jack Alberg, Christine Petersen, Julia Connolly, George Rasmussen, and Hanna Petersen; (third row, on gate) Jennie Coats, Catherine Petersen, and Dick Short. Work let up for dances, which lasted till early morning, but caring for the cows, horses, chickens, and pigs had to be done whether revelers had been up all night or not.

At the 1958 Danville Centennial parade, old-timers Cora Boone Root and Shelby Flournoy rode behind two white horses. The Flournoy family once owned the land east of San Ramon Creek in downtown Danville. Notice the lively young people sitting on top of the historic Hartz Avenue commercial buildings.

In that same parade, the grand marshal was five-term Congressman John F. Baldwin Jr., the popular scion of pioneers. He helped establish the Veteran's Hospital in Martinez and the I-680 freeway. His grandparents, Mary (Cox) and Robert O. Baldwin, arrived in the valley after the gold rush. Baldwin was the valley's congressman from 1955 to 1966.

This little parade may have been celebrating May Day. Helen Read is probably the adult supervising the gala event. In 1866, a joint May Day celebration with the San Ramon and Green Valley grammar schools featured a May pole decorated with flowers, a "flag which now floats in peace," and recitations from three May Queens—Louisa Hill, Laura Harlan, and Clara Glass.

One parade featured this verdant "float" advertising downtown Danville's Freitas and Peters Company, The Big Store. This prominent general store had doors both on Hartz and Prospect Avenues and wrapped around the San Ramon Valley Bank on the corner.

Fourth of July parties were celebrated at the Huntington Ranch near Mount Diablo, at Ramona Park, at Cox's Grove, and in downtown Danville during the 19th century. The current Danville Fourth of July parade began in 1962, when Virginia Deaton organized a pet parade, patriotic speeches, games for children, and fireworks. This color guard marched in 1989.

The old reservoir became Diablo Lake and was a popular spot for Mount Diablo Park Club members. There was a beach with fine sand, a raft, low and high diving boards, canoes, and flat-bottomed boats. It was stocked with fish. Sunbathing and beach side parties made the place complete.

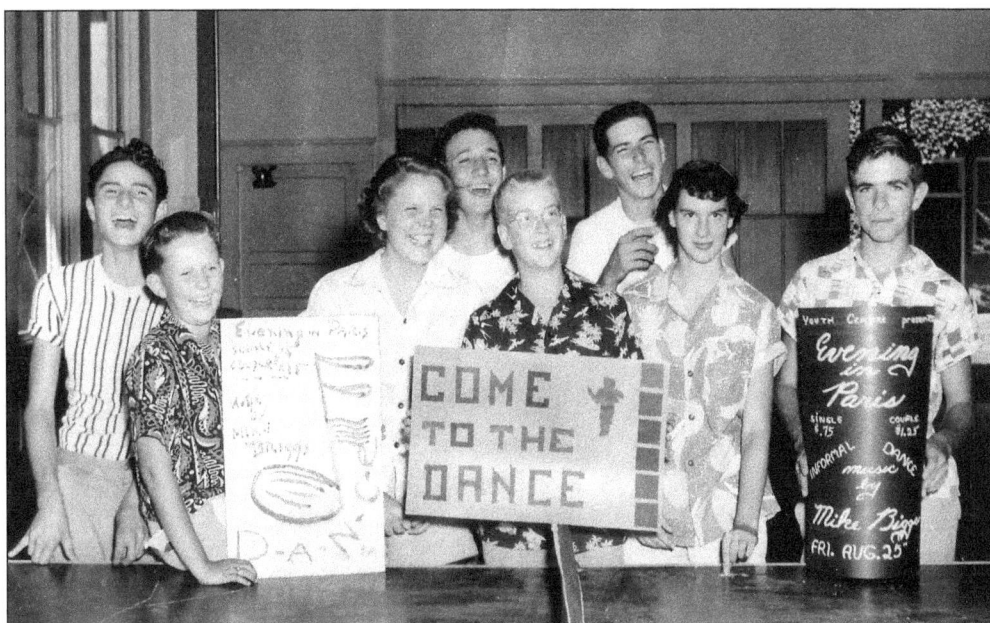

According to *The Valley Pioneer*, the San Ramon Valley Youth Center's last social event of the summer was "An Evening in Paris" held on August 25, 1950. Members of the dance committee, from left to right, are Tommy Santiago, Douglas Kirkpatrick, Ann Graham, Ronald Beach, Rob Polhemus, Ken Weaver, Judy McLain, and Terry Murphy.

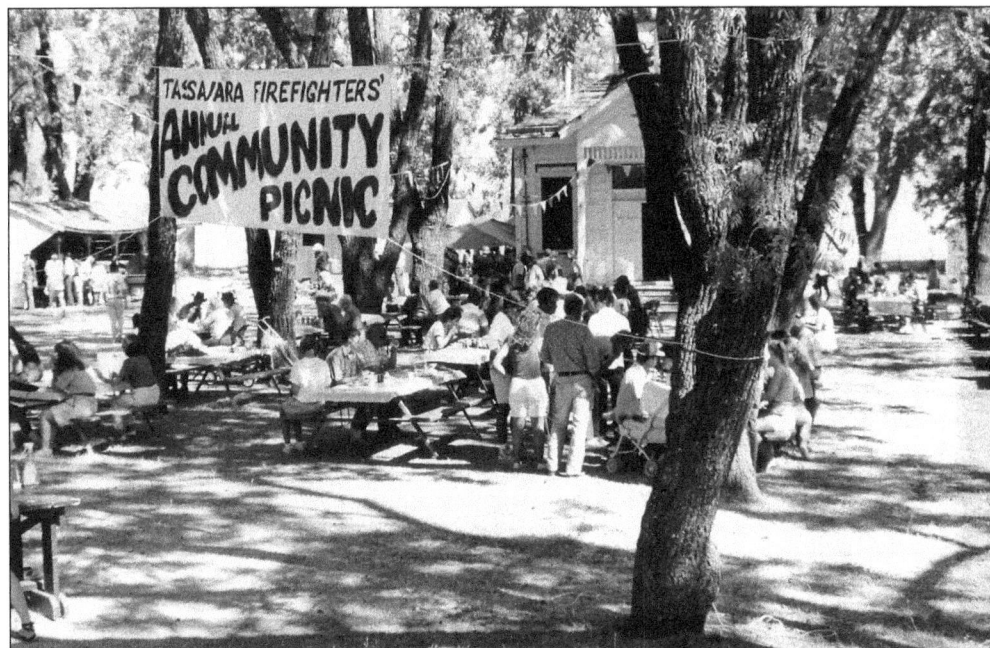

For years, the Tassajara firefighters and other volunteers hosted an annual community picnic at the Tassajara School House on Finley Road. Good food, good fellowship, and fund-raising to support the fire department were featured. One fire board member said that the picnic was their government. The classic school building is shown with the historic stable to one side around 1955.

Bill Fereira came back from the war with a bride, Violet Krga Fereira. On April 26, 1946, proud father William C. Fereira had a garden open house for the bride and groom. Greeting them, from left to right, are (first row) Violet and William J. Fereira, and little Gordon Beatty; (second row) Leo Norris III, Howard Wiedemann holding daughter Roxanne, Noel Norris, Tiny Peters, Robert Todoroff, and Wilbert Sousa; (third row) George Norris, Grace Norris, Everett Lynch, Doris Wiedemann, Mattie Wiedemann, Virgie Peters, Ramona (Lynch) Read, Mrs. Beatty, Susan (Lawrence) Todoroff, Newell Beatty, and Joe Lawrence.

Eight

RAILS AND ROADS

When the first train entered the valley in 1891, a reporter wrote, *"The beauty of the country seemed to increase as the train sped on (to Alamo)."* Danville *"is a thrifty locality with the modern tendency to progressiveness…".* At San Ramon *"the valley here broadens out, and is a very productive region."*

—*Contra Costa Gazette*, June 7, 1891

The gold and brown Danville depot in 1910 is a classic Southern Pacific building, complete with a roof finial and decorative knee braces. The Concord, Walnut Creek, and San Ramon depots were built in the same style. When the San Ramon Branch Line was built from Avon to San Ramon in 1891, it provided welcome passenger, mail, and freight service to residents. For a decade, from 1914 to 1924, the northern part of the valley had both steam and electric rail service. With the advent of the automobile, a local Good Roads League promoted paved roads for the valley.

This train is shown between Alamo and Danville. For years, valley residents lobbied for rail service. Finally Southern Pacific's Charles F. Crocker pledged to "blow his whistle in Danville" 60 days after SP received land for the track. In 1890, a committee composed of August Hemme, R. O. Baldwin, John A. Shuey, J. M. Stow, and Albert Glass contacted every landowner on the prospective right of way and secured the land.

This sugar beet chute was built at the Baldwin Ranch flag stop around 1900. A substantial siding allowed R. O. Baldwin to load hay, grain, and beets directly into a railroad car. Well known for his agricultural innovations, Baldwin planted 700 acres in sugar beets and added 80,000 fruit trees to his ranch. The flag stop was named Osage Station after trees he planted from seeds brought from Ohio, his home state.

The Alamo freight depot may have been modest in size, but it was a popular spot for people who wanted to visit friends and relatives. The distance from Alamo to San Francisco was 52.6 miles. Even in poor weather, patrons could use the train to come and go, a welcome relief from wagons, which sank into the adobe mud during the rainy season.

Alamo's freight depot was originally called "Hemme" and was located about one mile from the village center. The huge Hemme hay warehouse was near the depot. In 1939, this small depot, which measured only 20 feet by 40 feet, was dismantled.

SHUEY'S WAREHOUSES & RANCH. & S.P DEPOT. DANVILLE. J.A. SHUEY.

This *c*. 1895 drawing with Las Trampas hills to the west shows the Danville Depot and adjacent warehouses. Ranchers stored their grain and hay in the warehouses and were able to ship their products on demand. Fires in warehouses left their mark; in January 1893, one Shuey hay warehouse was completely destroyed by fire. Four thousand tons of hay were lost, and the depot was threatened.

Looking south, a train fronts one Danville warehouse. Significant new building activity took place in Danville because the station was so close to the downtown. New houses, hotels, businesses, warehouses, and boardwalks were constructed. There was less impact in Alamo, where the small freight depot was south of town and in San Ramon, where the village was one-half mile away from the depot.

A dapper group gets photographed near the depot. Hannah Hartz is in the center and Will Westerfield wears the derby. John and Catherine Hartz arrived in 1888 and purchased ranch land west of Danville. After the station was built, Hartz Ranch extended from the station land to Las Trampas hills.

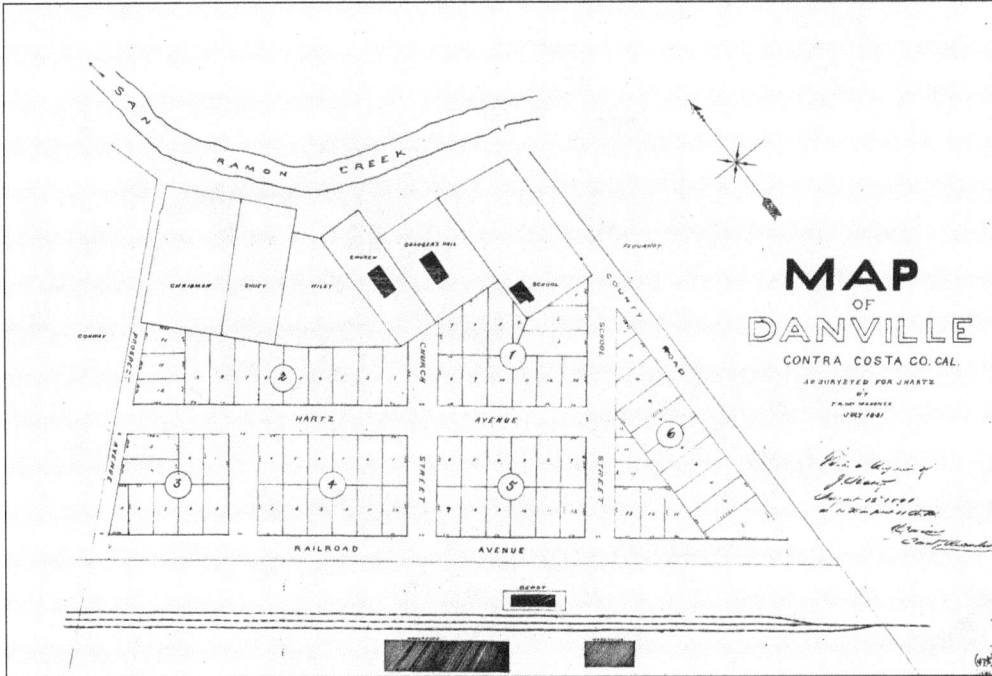

The Hartz addition was approved in July 1891, just one month after the first train came to the valley. John Hartz had deeded land for the right of way and sold Southern Pacific 8.65 acres for the Danville station land. This sale cut off his ranch land to the east. Seizing the opportunity, he subdivided the remnant piece, sold lots of 50 by 100 feet and 50 by 127 feet (some for $50), and created Hartz Avenue, Short, Church, and School streets.

The San Ramon "gallows" turntable and engine house was photographed about 1913. San Ramon was the end of the line from 1891 to 1909. The building was placed on a 910 foot-long spur and served as an overnight garage for the engine. After the engineer carefully balanced the engine on the turntable, crew and volunteers pushed it around.

The San Ramon depot was built in 1891 over one-half mile from the village of San Ramon. At first hotel keeper Frank Tinnin provided transportation between the depot and the village. After having several other names including Brevensville (for Levi Breven), Lynchville (for William Lynch), and Limerick (for Irish residents), San Ramon became the permanent name after the Branch Line arrived. In the 1920s, the depot was dismantled.

For a decade, the electric railway brought visitors to Mount Diablo and to a fashionable new country club created by R. N. Burgess, a Danville-raised entrepreneur. From 1914 to 1924, the electric railway was an easy way for tourists to reach Mount Diablo. To promote the new club, Burgess organized excursion trains which Alamo and Danville residents nicknamed "Million Dollar Specials."

The Oakland, Antioch & Eastern Railway (OA&E) served the northern part of the valley for a decade, hauling freight and passengers. Riders could use this railway to get to San Francisco, Chico, or Sacramento. Valley commuters rode it to Bay Point shipyards during World War I and nicknamed the train "The Riveter." Others fondly called it the "Toonerville Trolley" and recalled wild rides when the train was late.

Excursions on the train to Diablo were well-promoted by the Burgess publicity machine. One author wrote, "Opening of Mount Diablo Estate Sunday May 14, 1916 launched the most significant country home development in California. Three thousand visitors came on this opening day . . . They came by electric train and automobile and they left singing the praises of the Mount Diablo Estate." Residents could leave Diablo at 7:00 a.m. and arrive in San Francisco at 8:55 a.m.

Workers are building the electric railway track to Diablo through the wide-open spaces around 1914. Burgess owned 11,000 acres from near the summit to the foothills and persuaded the OA&E railway directors to extend the tracks to the new Mount Diablo Park Club. By 1916, the rails went along the present seventeenth and eighteenth golf fairways directly into the country club.

The Danville Branch of the San Ramon Valley bank building is flanked by the Freitas general store, pictured sometime between 1914 and 1924. Three types of transportation are shown: the horse, the car, and the electric railway. The first paved road went from Walnut Creek to Danville. On rainy days, unaware drivers would land abruptly in the mud after leaving Danville going south.

Oscar Olsson's garage was located on the northeast corner of Hartz Avenue and Diablo. His father, Andrew, had migrated from Sweden and ran a horse shoeing and general blacksmith store in San Ramon. Oscar, shown in the doorway with young Walter Elliott, opened a garage, Nash auto dealership, and service station in Danville. Involved with the volunteer fire service and other community activities, Oscar Olsson was elected county supervisor in the 1920s.

Ed Majors sits in front of the Myron Hall home with two Hall grandchildren, Lucy A. and Myron C. He is proudly driving a curved dash Oldsmobile, one of about 8,000 built from 1901 to 1905. Valley residents purchased cars and tractors as they became available, ending their total reliance on horses and rails. Many people recall the Chalmers, which the Wood brothers drove from their Sycamore Valley ranch to the new high school.

Some beaming car owners made it to the Mount Diablo summit on a "hill climb" around 1920. Automobile dealers touted their cars' trouble-free, record-breaking trips to Mount Diablo. Competitions were sponsored for the quickest trip from downtown Oakland to the summit, a 40-mile distance. In 1916, one adventuresome young lady, Lenore Barnett, drove a jazzy Maxwell roadster to the top and set a record of 1 hour, 45 minutes, and 5 seconds.

Nine

AGRICULTURE
A WAY OF LIFE

I have traveled the world and been in all the continents but have nowhere found such an Eden as this. This valley has a great future. All it needs is the booster spirit. We must put it on the map and let people know what we have here and then we will see a valley populated to its utmost with happy and contented people.

—W. J. Bond, *Contra Costa Courier*, 1914

Mount Diablo forms a backdrop as hay bales are loaded on a truck at Sycamore Valley's Wood Ranch around 1956. Agriculture was the business of the San Ramon Valley from the gold rush to the advent of suburban development. Farms and ranches covered the valley, with small village stores and blacksmith shops supporting them. Agriculture evolved from raising livestock, hay, and grain to cultivating grapes, almonds, apricots, plums, tomatoes, walnuts, and pears.

The National Grange, organized after the Civil War, gave rural families a chance to meet regularly and work collectively to influence decisions affecting agriculture. In 1873, the Danville Grange No. 85 was founded. This chromolithograph, printed in 1873 by Strobridge and Company, shows vignettes of farm activities. Grangers shared modern farm techniques, opposed high railroad shipping rates, and worked to eradicate ground squirrels.

Binders were used to cut, bundle, and tie stalks of grain and dump them in the field. Wagons would then collect the bundles and carry them to a stationary threshing machine. About 1916, this binder, pulled by a five-horse team, was cutting grain on the Donahue Ranch, which is now the Whitegate development.

Horses provided power to operate farm machinery. This threshing machine, operating on the Woodside Farm in the 1890s, used 15 horses. When driven in a circle, the slow rotary motion was converted through a series of gears to the high rotary motion needed by the threshing machine. From the 1860s to the 1890s, the valley's hard dry wheat went from Martinez ports to the Liverpool Corn Exchange, where it was highly valued.

The sack jig (man standing) used a wooden pole to settle the maximum amount of grain into the sack. Then he disconnected it from the hanger and set it in front of the sack-sewer. A clove hitch was used on the first ear and 12 stitches were taken across the top of the sack. The last ear was tied with two half-hitches.

Firewood was a profitable sideline product for farmers with fallen or excess trees, since almost every home needed stove wood for cooking and heating. Cooking was done on wood stoves before 1911, when electricity came to the valley.

A Caterpillar 60 tractor powers a Junior Monarch five-wire hay press in Green Valley around 1920. Hay presses of this type, powered by horses or by tractors, baled most of the hay in central California until 1945. The five-wire bales weighed about 250 pounds each. The conversion from horses to tractors reduced the need for so many farm laborers.

In the spring of 1910, Manuel and Mary Mattos came from the Azores and farmed in the Tri-Valley area, finally settling in the Tassajara Valley. The family, dressed in their Sunday best, poses with their prized animals. Pictured here, from left to right, are (first row) Frank, Max, Manuel Sr., twins Maro and Dolores, and Mary (behind cow), Manuel Jr., John, and sister Mary.

The Joneses in Alamo raised grapes on a large ranch in the early 1900s. Other small vineyards were planted in Stone Valley although there is no record of any large commercial wineries. During Prohibition in the 1920s, there were stills and bootleggers in Bollinger and Crow canyons and on Mount Diablo foothills.

109

A CONTRA COSTA COUNTY DAIRY.

In the 1887 *Pacific Rural Press*, Libbie Wood was quoted: "I have become quite an expert and run the separator without the aid of masculine assistance, although I allow my father and brothers to amuse themselves by keeping up the steam in the engine boiler for me sometimes. I am glad I can give a satisfactory report, for it would not do for the first lady who undertook the separator to fail as others might lose courage in attempting to operate what with us is proving so good a machine."

Cows were milked by hand until milking machines became available after 1900. Usually a cow would be put in a stanchion and fed grain while milking. Farmers churned cream to make butter and sold it in the surrounding communities. Butter from Woodside Farm was delivered and sold in Hayward once a week.

The Danville Creamery was located on the north side of School Street and Hartz Avenue from about 1900 to 1906. Viola Root recalled that "a Mr. George Lawrence had a truck and he would go to the ranches or dairies and gather the milk (cream) in big cans and bring the cans to the creamery to be made into butter."

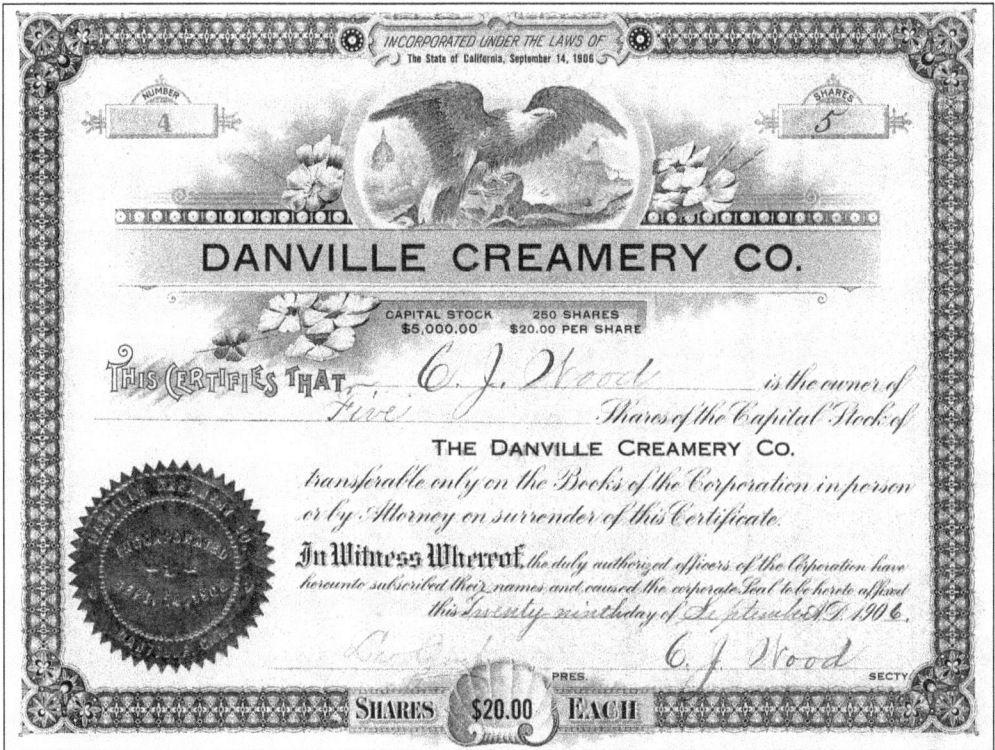

This Danville Creamery stock certificate was issued to Charles J. Wood for five shares at $20 each.

Fruits such as prunes and apricots were processed and laid out to dry in the sun, as shown in this 1934 Kuss Ranch picture. Several growers built gas-fired dehydrators, which greatly reduced the labor and time required to dry the fruit. Beginning in the 19th century, commercial orchards did very well in the valley. By the 1880s, apple, apricot, cherry, peach, pear, plum, and almond orchards were planted and producing fruit.

Plum trees are in spring bloom in an Alamo orchard during the 1930s. Plums were raised and dried for prunes throughout the San Ramon Valley. In the 20th century, acres of walnut trees thrived in the valley. Myron Ward Hall's first graft was dubbed the "Mother Tree" for the walnut industry in Contra Costa County.

Orchards still dominate the valley floor of Alamo in 1937. The large white building at the right of the picture is Bell's Store (3), located at Danville Boulevard and Las Trampas Road. Rancho-Romero can be seen at the upper right-hand side (2) in this picture. After World War II, the orchards were gradually sold for development.

The view from the Albert Glass Farm was to the northwest, across San Ramon. There are hay and grain fields with some of the Bishop Ranch orchards in the background. In the 20th century, the valley floor was full of open vistas such as this one.

Elizabeth and Caroline Anderson are framed by corn in a Tassajara field. When water could be obtained, a variety of crops were produced in the Tassajara Valley, although hay was always important. In later years, tomatoes were dry-farmed, often by Japanese-American farmers. The land between the plants was disked to encourage moisture and was not irrigated. People still recall these large, tasty tomatoes.

Bishop Ranch labels were applied to crates shipped from the ranch. In 1895, Thomas Benton Bishop acquired 3,000 acres of Norris ranch land in northwest San Ramon. In 1905, walnuts were planted and, in 1911, pears. Prizewinning Shropshire sheep were bred as well. By the 1920s, the ranch included 300 acres of walnuts, 280 acres of pears, 50 acres of vines, 20 of prunes, and 20 acres of peaches, plus 400 hogs and 100 cattle.

NET WEIGHT 46 LBS.

SAN RAMON

BRAND

CALIFORNIA
BARTLETT
PEARS

GROWN AND PACKED BY
THOMAS B. BISHOP CO.
SAN RAMON, CALIFORNIA.
PRODUCE OF U.S.A.

Bishop Ranch farm workers pose with their equipment in front of the walnut processing building about 1958. Pictured, left to right, are John Gilbride, Jim Allen, Superintendent Bob Livermore, foreman Al O'Shea, George Rose, mechanic Harry Steinmetz, Sonny O'Shea, Charles Smith, George Stegemann, Amos Yarge, Carlos Walker, and Livermore's dog Duke. In the 1950s, the ranch produced walnuts and pears, hay, grain, sheep, and hogs.

Four wells were developed in the 1930s to irrigate the Bishop Ranch pear orchard. Gated pipes were used to fill ditches that were realigned each year. In the late 1950s and 1960s, sprinklers were used to irrigate part of the walnut orchard as well. Vern Andreasen is showing his son Jim the irrigation system.

The first method of getting walnuts off the trees was with long poles. It was a miserable job—literally a pain in the neck.

Entire families helped pick walnuts. These women picked for the Boones. Because of labor shortages during World War II, local schools closed for a week so students could pick walnuts. City girl Ruth Boone organized all-women picking crews: "We never solicited a single orchard (to harvest). Everybody came to us and asked us if we'd take care of it. I had no more idea that I would end up doing a thing like that than flying to the moon!"

116

Christian Wiedemann bought this property off Norris Canyon Road in the 1860s. Family members still run cattle in the valley and hold annual roundups. The Wiedemanns own the Povis cattle brand (PS), which was first registered in 1856. It is one of the oldest registered brands in continuous use in California.

At the 1961 Wiedemann roundup, friends and neighbors gathered to rope and brand the calves born that year. Jeff Wiedemann wears the striped shirt and Howard Wiedemann is standing in the middle with a hat on. Usually there is more help than needed and a good party takes place after the work is done. Rodeos, to show off ranching skills, are a regular part of roundups.

In the 1930s, Black Angus cattle are grazing near today's Sycamore Valley Park; Short Ridge is in the background. According to one rancher, "Two slaughter houses served the Valley, Moller in Dublin and the Walnut Creek Meat Company on Ygnacio Valley Road. They purchased local animals and did custom slaughtering."

On Woodside Farm, a new 1918 Denby truck with solid rubber tires was loaded with 36 bales (4.5 tons) of hay.

118

Ten

MODERN PERSPECTIVES

After World War II the beauty of the valley drew new residents who moved into burgeoning developments and the new Round Hill Country Club. Change accelerated as the new interstate freeway opened first to Sycamore Valley Road and then to Dublin.

—Museum of the San Ramon Valley

1964 cartoon, when the freeway was opened to Sycamore Valley Rd.

VP FREEWAY SPECIAL, Oct. 28, 1964 PAGE 3

The much-anticipated interstate freeway opened from Walnut Creek to Danville's Sycamore Valley Road after a ceremony on November 1, 1964. Bill Hockins was grand marshal and pioneer descendant Claude Glass was honorary grand marshal. There was a ribbon cutting, an antique and modern car parade, and music by the San Ramon Valley High School band. After 1945, the San Ramon Valley was transformed from a rural community of just over 2,000 people to a suburban one. By 1970, there were 28,090 people in the valley. As new people moved in, modern road, water, and sewer systems were installed and schools, housing developments, and country clubs built. In the early 1980s, Danville and San Ramon incorporated and a major employment center, Bishop Ranch Business Park, opened.

Cameo acres

FURNISHED MODEL HOME OPEN DAILY

BED ROOM
BED ROOM
KITCHEN
LAUNDRY
BREEZEWAY
LIVING & DINING AREA
BED ROOM
GARAGE

DANVILLE'S LATEST HOME DEVELOPMENT
☆ TURN AT SHELL STATION ~ 2 MILES TO MODEL HOME

HERE IS WHAT YOU GET IN YOUR CAMEO ACRE HOME

FULL PRICE $9,350

VETERANS
$50 DOWN
...AND FIFTY DOLLARS CLOSING COSTS — SIXTY-SEVEN DOLLARS MONTHLY INCLUDES TAXES AND INSURANCE.

NON-VETERANS
$1650 DOWN
...AND FIFTY DOLLARS CLOSING COSTS — FIFTY-EIGHT DOLLARS MONTHLY INCLUDES TAXES AND INSURANCE.

☆ THREE BEDROOMS
☆ QUARTER ACRES
☆ NEW FRONT LAWN
☆ BRICK FIRE PLACE
☆ COPPER PLUMBING
☆ REAL TILE BATH
☆ KITCHEN TILE
☆ WARDROBE CLOSETS
☆ STEEL CASEMENTS
☆ HARDWOOD FLOORS

☆ TWO WALL FURNACES
☆ CEDAR SHINGLES
☆ LARGE BREEZEWAY
☆ CHOICE OF COLORS
☆ ELEC. BATH HEATER
☆ COUNTRY LIVING
☆ SWIMMING POOL
☆ KIDDIES' PLAY AREA
☆ SCHOOL BUS AT DOOR
☆ WINDOW SCREENS

☆ TURN AT SHELL STATION ~~~ DANVILLE
KIRBY HUGHES REALTY CO. 8536 MAC ARTHUR BLVD.
TR 2-3726 - DIABLO 153 W

George Jovick purchased 350 acres of the Macomber Ranch in 1946 and sold two-acre lots for custom homes. The subdivision was called Montair and it was the first large home development in the valley after World War II. Pat Offield, who worked on the Montair project, looks across the rural valley to Mount Diablo. The California Water Company provided the water.

During the 1950s, new subdivisions were built in Danville, including Montair, Danville Gardens, Montego, Danville Estates, Cameo Acres, Vista Grande, and San Ramon Heights. The Cameo Acres homes were built from models on lots of one-fourth to one-third acres, a new type of development for the rural valley.

120

In 1960, Round Hill Country Club was dedicated by torching a gold-plated chain. Pictured, from left to right, are Art Honegger, Mel Whalen, Harlan Geldermann, Buck Connors, county supervisor Mel Nielsen (with the torch), Joe Silva, Joseph H. Dwilla, John Sparrowk, and Bill Hockins (in back with the bow tie). John Sparrowk and Harlan Geldermann developed the club, buying rolling ranch lands owned by the Mott sisters and Grover Squier. In 1961, club memberships cost $1,700.

Families began moving into San Ramon Village—advertised as the "Wonderful World of San Ramon"—after this dedication in July 1960. Developers Ken Volk and Robert McLain purchased 4,300 acres of valley land in Alameda and Contra Costa Counties, with help from real estate agent Harlan Geldermann. An entire city rose from the ranch lands, including over 10,000 homes, shopping centers, and golf courses. Home prices ranged from $14,000 to $30,000.

September 24, 1966, was "DD Days," celebrating the freeway extension from Danville to Dublin. Pictured, from left to right, are, Wilson Close, Allen S. Hart, Mrs. Hart, Al Kaplan, and an unidentified girl. The first new Volk-McLain homes called "San Ramon Village" were actually built in Dublin. New and old residents living in the valley were happy to leave the congested Danville Highway for a new interstate.

Arguments over the new freeway alignment resonated across the valley. Here San Ramon's Brass Door (once known as the 8/5 club) is shown next to the old highway. The large building in the center was cut in half by the new freeway. Bishop Ranch hay warehouses can be seen to the east.

Sworn in by Superior Court Judge Max Wilcox Jr., Danville's first council members, from left to right, are Mayor John May, Beverly Lane, Dick McNeely, Susanna Schlendorf, and Doug Offenhartz. Danville went to the ballot on June 8, 1982, and voters supported a new town—5,809 to 4,952. The new town council tackled local issues for a population of 26,445. Improved planning, police, roads, and parks were goals for the first council.

Celebrating a successful election is the first San Ramon City Council: Mary Lou Oliver, Mayor Diane Schinnerer, Rick Harmon, Wayne Bennett, and Jerry Ajlouny. With Dublin and Danville incorporating the year before, San Ramon voters were ready for their own city. On March 8, 1983, by a vote of 3,825 to 1,254, San Ramon incorporated with a population of 22,356. While Bishop Ranch Business Park was not part of the incorporated boundaries, it was soon annexed to the new city.

Bishop Ranch was still an agricultural enterprise in the 1970s. In 1978, Sunset Development Company purchased 585 acres of the ranch and developed light industry and modern offices in the new Bishop Ranch Business Park. Developers Masud and Alex Mehran kept the name "Bishop Ranch" as a tribute to its history. In 1985, from left to right, are businesses Toyota (large rectangular building), Pacific Bell (crescent lake), and Chevron, shown east of I-680.

Bishop Ranch Business Park evolved into one of the largest business parks in California, with headquarters for Pacific Bell (later SBC) and Chevron, totaling 8.5 million square feet of office space with a potential work force of 30,000. Its impact on the valley has been profound. Cutting the ribbon for the Bollinger Canyon interchange in 1985, from left to right, are Tony Dehaesus, Christina Mehran, Masud Mehran, Larry Dahms, Tom Powers (behind scissors), Ed DeSilva, Alexander Mehran, Leo McCarthy, Burch Bachtold, and Mike Walford. The children are Annabel and Alexander Mehran Jr.

124

Standing around this billboard, from left to right, are Tony Cicero, John May, and Bill Hockins. The sign was located at the south end of Danville. After Danville centennial celebrations in 1958, Russel Glenn, Tom Ohlson, and others took a good look at the downtown, which had been dubbed "Gasoline Alley" by some wags. The Confederacy of Danville was proclaimed and merchants were encouraged to "create a town with a pleasing personality."

Eugene and Carlotta O'Neill lived in Tao House in the valley's western hills from 1937 to 1944. Here the renowned playwright wrote his final, great plays, including A Moon for the Misbegotten, The Iceman Cometh, and Long Day's Journey into Night. This national historic site is now owned by the National Park Service. The Eugene O'Neill Foundation helped save the house and provides programs promoting O'Neill's legacy.

Forest Home Farms Historic Park began in 1997, when Ruth Quayle Boone donated 16 acres of land to the City of San Ramon. To commemorate the area's agricultural past, San Ramon operates the park and provides programs and events for children and adults. It is a national historic site. Numa and Minnie Boone built this Dutch Colonial house shortly after they married in 1900; their property once extended across the valley.

In 1972, most of the 6,500-acre Blackhawk Ranch was sold to developer Kenneth Behring, who planned to subdivide the land to build 4,800 homes. It was the largest single housing development ever proposed in the county and was very controversial. Only 2,400 homes were approved on 4,200 acres, and over 2,000 acres of foothill land were donated to Mount Diablo State Park. Blackhawk Plaza and the Blackhawk Automotive Museum (shown above) were built in the 1980s.

The restored Danville Southern Pacific Depot is now the Museum of the San Ramon Valley. A national historic site, it was moved to its present location in 1996. The museum provides historical information through exhibits, a research library, archives, speakers, and school programs. Docent tours of the museum, Old Town Danville, and the Alamo Cemetery are provided.

The Tassajara Grammar School, built in 1889, served its community until 1946. Each spring, third grade students learn what life was like in a one-room school, taught by Museum of the San Ramon Valley docents. The school property is owned and operated by the San Ramon Valley Fire Protection District. In 1999, docents Patty Connett (left) and Joan Kurtz (second from the right) stand with a class of third-graders from Vista Grande School.

BOOKS ABOUT THE
SAN RAMON VALLEY

Blackmur, Arnold. *In Old Diablo, A Social History*. Redwood City, CA: Ampex Corporation, 1981.

Dotson, Irma M. *Danville Branch of the Oakland Antioch & Eastern Railway*. Danville, CA: Museum of the San Ramon Valley, 1996.

————. *San Ramon Branch of the Southern Pacific*. Danville, CA: Museum of the San Ramon Valley, 1991.

Dotson, Irma M. and James M. Dotson. *Downtown Danville, Changes in 25 Years, 1976–2001*. Danville, CA: Irma M. Dotson, 2001.

Drummond, G. B., ed. *Recollections, Early Life in the San Ramon Valley as related by Prof. James Dale Smith*. Oakland, CA: GRT Book Printing, 1995.

Emery, Rose Peters. *Footprints in the Soil, A Portuguese-Californian Remembers*. San Jose, CA: Portuguese Heritage Publications, 2003.

Jones, Virgie V. *Be It Ever so Humble*. Alamo, CA: Morris-Burt Press, 1983.

————. *Historical Persons and Places . . . in San Ramon Valley*. Alamo, CA: Morris-Burt Press, 1977.

————. *Remembering Alamo . . . and Other Things Along the Way*. Alamo, CA: Morris-Burt Press, 1975.

Stone, James C. *Diablo's Legacy, Recollections & Reflections, 1912–Present*. San Francisco, CA: Miller Freeman Inc., 1994.

Tatam, Robert Daras. *Old Times in Contra Costa*. Pittsburg, CA: Highland Publishers, 1996.

Visit us at
arcadiapublishing.com

· ·

www.ingramcontent.com/pod-product-compliance
Lightning Source LLC
Chambersburg PA
CBHW050550110426
42813CB00008B/2315